Route 66 Traveler's Guide
and Roadside Companion

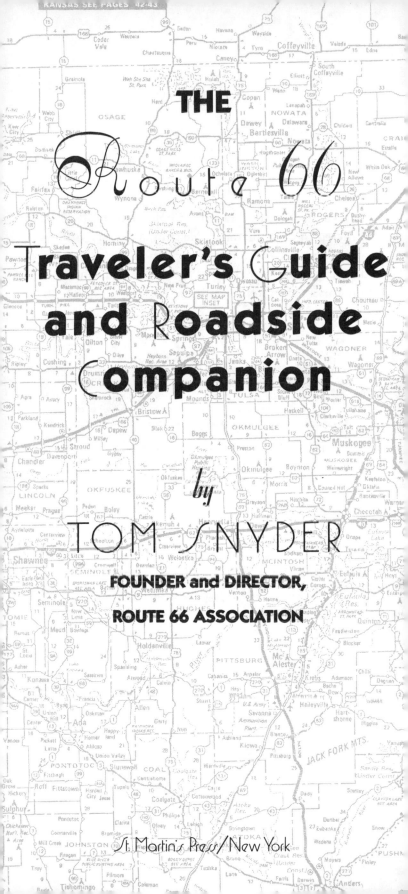

THE
Route 66
Traveler's Guide and Roadside Companion

by

TOM SNYDER

FOUNDER and DIRECTOR,
ROUTE 66 ASSOCIATION

St. Martin's Press/New York

A NOTE TO THE READER

You will notice a few advertisements from the 1930s
scattered throughout this guide. Although none of these
businesses are to be found along the old highway today,
the ads provide something of the charm and allure of
way-back-then travel over Route 66.

Design by Glen M. Edelstein

Library of Congress Cataloging-in-Publication Data

Snyder, Tom, 1934–
        The Route 66 traveler's guide / Tom Snyder : introduction by
    Michael Wallis.
            p.   cm.
        ISBN 0-312-04587-5
        1. United States—Description and travel—1981-   —Guide-
        books.
        2. United States Highway 66—Guide-books.   I. Title.   II. Title:
    Route sixty-six traveler's guide.
    E158.S986   1990
    917.304′928—dc20   90-37195
                                                                              CIP

First Edition: November 1990
10   9   8   7   6   5   4   3   2   1

DEDICATED to my mother and father—and all parents —who lovingly offer to wide-eyed kids the wonders of a mystical journey to California on Route 66. And to my good friend Jack Rittenhouse, whose marvelous little road book has guided so many of us safely there.

CONTENTS

ACKNOWLEDGMENTS

My heartfelt appreciation goes to Howard Goetzman and Janice Vandeventer for their continuing support of this work; to Don Davenport, whose all-hours computer wizardry and everyday humanity made the digitized maps possible; and to the road crew of Jim Powell and JoAnne Vervinck, who, by driving and even walking abandoned sections of roadway, helped to confirm the location and present condition of uncounted old alignments.

I am similarly indebted to Peter Egan and Len Frank for early inspiration and personal encouragement, and to Travis Brooks, Richard Weingroff, Tom Smith, Mary Hanel, and Chris Schwarberg, for their enthusiastic research efforts.

Thanks also go to the Departments of Tourism in each of the Route 66 states, and especially to Judi Snow, Mary Kay Cline, Bart Ripp, Sally Ferrell, Angel Delgadillo, Jerry Richard, Ron Chavez, and Sean Bersell, who recognized, as individuals, the deeper value of a Route 66 revival.

To Mike McCarville, Maxine Wilhelm, Bob Capps, Tom Higley, Melody Kellogg, Carolyn Howard, Jamie Wise, Vicki Covey, Tommy Thompson, Lloyd Combs, Tommy Pike, Dan Stark, Maggie Ivy, Jeanette Koenig, and Toby Diane Aswal, my gratitude for sharing their resources, their road stories, and themselves.

Special thanks go to my editor, longtime Route 66 fan Bob Weil; to designer Glen Edelstein, together with editors Andrea Connolly and Bill Thomas, for their talents, graciousness, and attention to every detail; to my agent, Suzanne Fitzgerald Wallis; and to confirmed roadie and fellow author Michael Wallis. A writer could not ask for greater support on any project nor wish for better friends.

And, finally, I am especially grateful to the hundreds of members of the national Route 66 Association—across the country, in Europe, and in Asia —who supported a portion of the research on which the substance of this guide rests.

INTRODUCTION

U.S. Route 66 was stamped on the American public's consciousness in 1926. That was the year the fabled highway was christened. Through the decades this remarkable road has been celebrated in song and literature. Route 66 became an escape route for Dust Bowl pilgrims, a thoroughfare for troop convoys bound for war, and the most popular highway in the country for droves of tourists.

A ribbon that tied the nation together, Route 66's concrete and asphalt pavement snaked across eight states. It was known as America's Main Street.

It still is.

Although five interstate superslabs attempted to kill off the Mother Road, the old highway is still there. In some stretches it may be only a service road or a fragment that runs off into the weeds. In other parts of the country it truly remains the best way to go.

Route 66 has evolved into a venerable veteran. It is a timeless monument to the people who live and work on the edges of the highway and the legions of motorists who travel its length.

State and national organizations, all dedicated to seeing that Route 66 survives, are actively promoting the Mother Road. Yet despite the continued interest in the protection and preservation of the historic highway, Route 66 is unquestionably not for everybody

Route 66 is clearly not a path for people in a hurry. Nor is it for those whose palates are accustomed only to homogenized food and drink. And it is certainly not for those who prefer the predictable or who shy away from anything that hints of old-fashioned fun. Those folks had better stick to the turnpikes and interstates.

Route 66 is for a special breed.

It's for travelers willing to slow the pace just to watch the sun sizzle on the horizon. It's for those who are willing to sample chili from a stranger's pot, slurp root beer floats out of frosty mugs, or tackle a burger platter that requires at least a dozen napkins to sop grease off hands and chin.

It's for those able to fall asleep in a motel bed lulled by the tattoo of eighteen-wheelers' tires on the pavement. It's for folks who would rather drive through the heart of a small town than make time on the interstate. It's for those for whom the vacation begins the moment they back out of the driveway, opting for frequent stops to peek inside a snake pit, thumb through racks of postcards, or paw over curios. It's for the people who will always be suckers for neon lights and home-cooked meals.

I like to put it this way—Route 66 is for people who find time holy. That about sums it up.

Tom Snyder, founder of the national Route 66 Association, finds his time very holy. That's obvious after you spend only a minute with him. Tom makes the most of his time and yours. It's a blessing to be cherished and the sweetest gift of all.

In this comprehensive guidebook to Route 66, Tom, one of the old highway's most valiant champions, offers all true aficionados of the Mother Road not only a workable blueprint to adventure but a prescription for making the best use of their time.

In 1946, Jack Rittenhouse paved the way and did all open-road travelers a favor by assembling his folksy Route 66 guidebook. For decades, that slim booklet was the standard. Rittenhouse served as a scout and provided useful hints about where to dine and sleep and what to see and do along the way. He gave practical tips to make the trip tolerable.

Tom goes a bit further. He makes the journey an event to savor every mile of the way. He draws from his own experiences and observations as he leads travelers on an odyssey down the best-known highway in the world.

Route 66 Traveler's Guide and Roadside Companion, superbly illustrated with vintage maps overlaid with interstate routes, should be owned by anyone even remotely interested in experiencing up close and personal an American corridor that has managed to beat the clock and survive.

It's ideal for anyone who finds time holy.

—MICHAEL WALLIS
Author of *Route 66: The Mother Road*

WELCOME TO
THE OLD ROAD

Traveling is about seeing new places, and about pointing a camera at squinting people or at things that usually turn out to be too far away.

Traveling is about spending money on stuff you'd never dream of buying at home. It's about discovering the different and occasionally the bizarre—about finding something adventurous, daring, and even romantic in yourself. It's about expanding your perceptions along with the changing view just beyond the windshield.

Traveling is like racy lingerie, trashy magazines, kitchen gadgets, and auto accessories. None of these are truly necessary, but they all make life a little more interesting, a little spicier than it might otherwise be. Old Route 66 is like that. No longer necessary to efficient cross-country travel, the road has been replaced by five seamless interstate highways with no stoplights, no places of special interest, no appealing monstrosities. Just mile-by-mile progress in one direction or another. After the first few hours the ordinariness of it all is like watching a test pattern on television.

But Route 66—ah, Route 66 was never ordinary. From its commissioning in 1926, the first highway to link Chicago with Los Angeles, US 66 was, to townspeople along the route and travelers alike, something special. Soon it was even being called the "most magical road in all the world." And by any standard, that's what it became.

Swinging southwest by west from Lake Michigan, US 66 crossed the rivers, plains, mountains, deserts, and canyons of eight states and several Native American nations before ending 2,448 miles later on a bluff above the Pacific. Yet like most American highways of the day, the original roadway remained little more than a dusty, transcontinental rut that usually filled with water and mud on the least occasion of rain. In those days, even Lindbergh's solo flight over the Atlantic was easier than a cross-country trek by automobile in the same year. Travelers who made it as far as the Great Mojave paid dearly to load their vehicles onto railroad flatcars rather than risk a breakdown out on the vast desert.

Still, the road that became America's Main Street was nothing if not commercially inspired. An intense lobbying effort by the original US Highway 66 Association soon created, from a patchwork of farm-to-market roads and old trails, a single, all-weather highway. More importantly, the Association transformed that highway into something else as well: *the idea that Route 66 is an extraordinary experience—a destination in itself.*

That idea is what changed a more convenient way to cross the country into a new purpose for going. A few days' travel on Route 66 became a tour of the highway itself and the excitement of being on the road became as important as any arrival. In advertising terms, that's when the sizzle caught up with the steak.

By the mid-1930s, the highway had begun to create its own myth; it grew larger than life. It became *the* way west. First it was John Steinbeck, who recognized a feminine, nurturing quality in Route 66, and termed it "the mother road," forever embedding the highway and the Joad family in the nation's consciousness. After World War II, it was Bobby Troup's turn. His musical Triptik for getting your kicks on Route 66 has since been recorded by nearly everyone from the Andrews Sisters to the Rolling Stones and Michael Martin Murphey. But it was the first great recording by Nat King Cole that changed the way an entire nation would pronounce the name. After Cole's rendition, it would be "root sixty-six" forever. During the 1960s, the road became even more famous, earning top billing in the literate and successful TV series *Route 66*, created by Stirling Silliphant and Herbert B. Leonard and propelled across the continent by Nelson Riddle's magnificent road theme.

In the process, US 66 became much more than a

highway. For the millions who traveled her (and the millions more who still want to), the road was transformed from a concrete thoroughfare into a national symbol: a vital life-sign for us all. A pathway to better times—seldom found, but no less hoped for. Route 66 came to represent not only who we were as a people, but who we knew we could be. Not a bad thing to find in a road.

Yet change came to old Route 66, as to all who traveled her. She was abandoned in many places, reduced to the homely duties of "frontage road" in others, her magic double digits were given away, her job taken over by a homogenized, fast-food freeway. With the final stretch of I-40 opened in 1984, and the decision by state transportation officials to remove all trace of US Route 66 markings, the upbeat road rhythms became a dirge. And this time we risk losing a great deal more than just another obsolete highway— this time we risk losing something of ourselves.

But there ought to be a saying that you can't keep a good road down. You may take away her destination, even steal her magic numbers. But you can't keep old Route 66 out of the hearts and thoughts of three generations of road-borne Americans.

All across the country and even beyond, there's a groundswell of popular interest in old Route 66. Along the grand old highway, local townspeople are recognizing a deeper, more enduring interest among travelers who want the experience of driving America's Main Street again. State and local Route 66 associations have organized from Chicago to Los Angeles, and the national Route 66 Association, formed in 1983, continues to expand its work. National legislation, authored and introduced by Senator Pete V. Domenici of New Mexico, also strongly supports the revitalization effort. And so can you.

Just by driving the old road and visiting with the truly wonderful people to be found along the way, you'll become part of the spirit and the legacy of Route 66 across America. As you follow the vintage road maps in this book, you'll find the thin, wavy line that was once Route 66 seems frail, often cut completely through by the double-barreled interstate.

But there's a lot of fire and an embracing warmth in the grand old lady yet. So take everything in, experience the road fully, be a part of what you find. Enjoy every curve, every long, die-cut straight, every place to stop along the way. Re-create for yourself and share with those you love the sweetness of a time gone by. A time to be rediscovered on America's Main Street. Welcome to the old road.

Welcome to Route 66.

ABOUT THIS
TRAVELER'S GUIDE

A Brief
Look Back

Most of us think of the Auto Club in terms of a
magical plastic card that can get us out of the soup
when the battery dies on a rainy Monday morning, or
when that baldish, left rear tire finally goes flat
somewhere west of Barked Knuckle. That's truly
unfortunate. Because there is much more to the Auto
Club story, and a rich history to boot.

Except for a handful of urban operations and small
automotive social clubs, the Automobile Club of
Southern California was virtually alone when it was
established as a service organization in 1900. Aviation,
radio, television, balloon tires, the tin lizzie—tow
trucks, certainly—were all in the future. Even the
ubiquitous American Automobile Association (AAA) did
not make an appearance for another two years.

Indeed, at a time when most road maps were little
more than by-guess-and-by-gosh squiggles, the
Automobile Club of Southern California was already
making highly detailed surveys of major roadways in the
United States. Beginning in 1920, the Club undertook
charting of both the National Old Trails and Lincoln
highways from Los Angeles to New York City and
Washington, D.C. Using a roadster equipped with a
survey speedometer, compass, inclinometer, and
altimeter, a crew of two documented an amazing 25,000
miles of highway in the first year and an equal number
in 1921.

The strip maps you see in this guide are based on

later refinements of that first—and to this day, astonishing—undertaking by the Automobile Club of Southern California. Today, using the latest in electronic survey methods and digital technology, the Automobile Club of Southern California continues as a major resource in cartographic development.

One last note: Remember that the 1930s ads found throughout this guide are for businesses no longer in operation along the route.

Using These Vintage Maps

Each map you find here is a superb example of the cartographer's art. Every representation, with its detailed landforms, rivers, ponds, structures, roadways, and towns, can be invaluable in rediscovering many portions of old (or old, old) Route 66, which have been retired for thirty years or more. Even major railroads sometimes move or disappear altogether. But mountains, valleys, and (most) rivers pretty well stay put, and these maps show them clearly. So you're sure to enjoy tracking down the parts of old Route 66 that interest you most, using these maps as your guide. Even in this day of satellite photography and computer enhancement, these beautifully crafted little strips remain a marvel of both information and accuracy.

To assist you in making transitions from the superhighways to old Route 66, *the approximate routes of related interstates—appearing as dotted lines with I-numbering —have been superimposed on the original map bases through special computer processing*. A few nonexistent or ruined portions of old Route 66 have also been deleted where these might be confusing.

Otherwise, each of the strip maps appears here just as it did when originally published. Most are from the 1933 edition of *National Old Trails Road and U.S. Highway 66*. The Santa Rosa–Albuquerque section is drawn from a booklet published after that alignment was completed in 1937. A separate strip map is also used to cover the last segment from Los Angeles to Santa Monica, not included in the 1933 publication.

Your Route 66 Tour

If you're one of the many who have tired of the interstate grind, this guide will introduce you to easy-on easy-off sections of old Route 66. At first, you may have only a couple of hours to spare. That's fine. But if you love the feeling of an old two-lane road, if you want the experience of going back to an earlier time, if you are like the rest of us—travelers who have become enchanted by Route 66—you'll soon be back for the whole tour. In the meantime, it's always fun to do a little mind traveling.

This guide was not designed for coffee-table conversation, however. It will serve you best when kept in the glove compartment or close at hand. It should be well thumbed, brown edged, and stained with juices from your favorite Route 66 cafes and barbecue joints. And if the back cover ends up as a shim for a noisy side window, so much the better. When the pages get really bad, just have the whole thing bronzed. It might be a good way to memorialize all your experiences along the old road.

One further suggestion: if you're not an Auto Club member already, you may want to consider joining. Their exhaustive tour book listings of accommodations, plus the excellent regional maps they offer, are worth more than the price of an annual membership. And you get the tow truck for free.

Remember only that too much dependence on toll-free reservations and such can deaden the feeling of personal adventure, romance, and discovery that comes with exploring an old road on your own. The aim in this guide is to achieve a balance between touring commentary and your right to find your own way, make your own discoveries, and choose when you need to make time on the interstate. And when you don't.

Even if you're only a closet roadie, you'll be delighted to know that with few exceptions, old Route 66 can still carry you from Lake Michigan to the California coast. Most of the towns and much of the original roadway remains, and you'll enjoy seeing the country as you may never have seen it before. You'll also enjoy meeting many of the people who have made this highway their life. They're good folks.

Be sure to say hello for all of us.

Route 66 Traveler's Guide and Roadside Companion

CHAPTER

|

Illinois

It's tempting to think of old Route 66,
stretching from Chicago to Los Angeles, as
a happy accident. After all, her famous
double-sixes were little more than that, the
road having first been designated Route 60
for a short time. But the truth is that there
is a strong Illinois–California connection
that predates the road, extending back to
the turn of the century. It was then that
the route which was to become US 66 was
cobbled together from existing pathways.
And they really were little more than
pathways. Trails, traces, fence-row tracks,
farm-to-market roads, and even some
private drives were linked with stagecoach
routes farther west to create something
resembling a continuous roadway. And just
in time, too, for the unending stream of tin
lizzies being mass-produced by Henry Ford.

Business and personal connections
between Chicago and Los Angeles were
already established as well. One of
Hollywood's very first moviemakers came

not from New York but from Chicago. The winter of
1907 had threatened to run Francis Boggs and his tiny
film company out of business. Only the interior scenes
of Boggs's twelve-minute epic, *The Count of Monte Cristo,*
had been shot when the snows ended any hope of
outdoor filming. Boggs, his crew, and his players headed
west in search of better conditions and a light more
suited to the slow film speeds of the day. They found
what they needed in Los Angeles—bright sunshine,
cheap land, and free scenery. The following year Boggs
moved production to the West Coast for good. Ince,
Sennett, DeMille, and others followed, of course, but
Chicagoan Boggs had led the way. Even the name
Hollywood came not from the holly trees that were
planted later but from an upstate neighborhood in
Illinois.

Of the midwestern states, Illinois has always
been the champion trader, track layer, and road
builder, with Chicago at its hub—importing and
exporting anything movable, anything thinkable. But
Chicago need not have lured itself into the trap of
comparison. Better to be called Windy City than
Second City. For there is nothing whatever second
class about Chicago. Its outrageous blend of southern
black cool, northern liberalism, and blue-collar ethic,
along with its midwestern reserve and commercial
might, is sometimes politically awkward—but always
in motion.

None can fan the twin flames of devotion and
despair quite like the Cubbies. And even Green Bay
cannot match the chill factor at Soldier Field during a
Bears losing streak. Chicago has exported broad-
shouldered poetry, prairie architecture, miles of
unfortunate hams, uncounted Studs Terkelisms, a large
part of the original cast of *Saturday Night Live,* plus—bet
you didn't know this—the Lava Lite, premier icon of
the early-plastic 1960s.

These are good things to know, if you're starting
out on a tour of old Route 66 from its beginning point.
For, in a very real sense, Los Angeles could not have
been successfully linked with the eastern seaboard. Even
with today's bicoastal management style, Southern
California and New York have too little in common.

Only Chicago—hunkered down, smack in the middle of America's heartland—could anchor one end of a great, new westering highway that factory workers, farmhands, hitchhikers, businesspeople, teachers, truckers, and songwriters would know as their own. Chicago was, and is, exactly the right place to start.

Chicago to Bloomington

First, let's clear up some confusion about the origin of the highway in downtown **Chicago.** Old Route 66 originally began on Jackson Boulevard at Michigan Avenue, a few blocks north of the present-day departure of Interstate (I) 55 from I-90 and 94. After the 1933 World's Fair provided some reclaimed land, the terminus was moved farther east to Lake Shore Drive at the entrance to Grant Park. Then, in 1955, Jackson Boulevard became an eastbound one-way thoroughfare with Adams Street as its westbound counterpart, one block farther north. So the most direct route west is now via the newer Adams alignment.

After just a few blocks, you'll be driving between two of Chicago's greatest landmarks—sites that would ultimately serve to propel generations of Americans down old Route 66.

A few blocks to the north, at Des Plaines and Randolph Streets, is the site of the Haymarket tragedy. There, near the turn of the century, a group of what were then called *anarchists* were demonstrating for the eight-hour workday and against police brutality in suppressing the movement toward decent conditions in the workplace. A bomb was thrown—even today no one knows by whom—resulting in the deaths of both police and demonstrators. Organizers were tried and convicted in a biased court and most were hanged almost immediately with no chance for appeal. It was this country's first Red scare as well as a beginning of

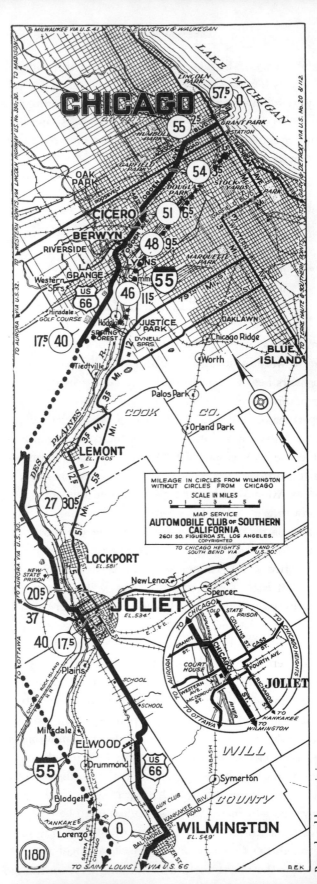

the American industrial reform movement.

Just a few blocks in the opposite direction, on Halstead Street below Polk, is Hull House, Jane Addams's pioneering settlement project. Seeing the effects of industrial poverty and immigrant exploitation, Addams established an on-site program for whole families and neighborhoods, providing the first child care, social welfare, and adult education for the poor. As with the labor movement and the later Dust Bowl migrations, the settlement houses fueled a large part of the later westward expansion along old Route 66, as urban industry collapsed during the early years of the Depression.

From Adams, just beyond Ashland Avenue, take Ogden Avenue southwest through **Cicero.** Once a home away from home for Chicago mobsters, Cicero's streets were honeycombed with tunnels allowing gangsters and bootleggers to move unseen from blind pig to brothel, with even Eliot Ness and his Untouchables none the wiser. Cicero now works hard to present a squeaky-clean image. Almost too squeaky. But some of the tunnels are still there. Perhaps there's even one right under the intersection of Ogden and Cicero Avenues. In any event, continue on through **Berwyn,** jog south on Harlem Avenue, which is State Route (SR) 43 in Lyons, and turn southwest again on Joliet Road.

Since I-55 has largely been constructed on top of old Joliet Road, you'll be obliged to join the interstate. Exit the interstate at Joliet Road south to follow the old route into **Joliet.** A later alignment of Route 66 once passed through **Plainfield** as well. There is little to recommend it, though. Continue on SR 53 through Joliet or, if you wish to skirt the city, stay on I-55 to the Wilmington exit.

South to **Wilmington,** the route is mostly newer four-lane highway. A bit north of Elwood, however, across a small bridge, an older two-lane alignment swings off to the east. Watch for the line of weathered telephone poles—frequently the sign of an older alignment—and continue on Manhattan Road to Mississippi Road, curving back toward SR 53. Rounding the bend, the two-lane becomes Elwood Road and recrosses the newer highway. Continue west on the old alignment into **Elwood** proper. Then follow Douglas until it rejoins SR 53 at the southern end of town.

After entering Wilmington, follow the old route west on Baltimore (SR 53) and continue south through **Braidwood, Godley,** and **Braceville.** Some of the first landmarks of old Route 66 appear along this stretch of two-lane highway, along with several beer-and-skittles roadhouses. South of **Gardner,** as SR 53 swings back north, make a hard left turn to the south and continue on the old two-lane alignment of Route 66. Or continue south to Bloomington on I-55, which closely parallels this route.

Four-lane bypasses for the towns from **Dwight** through **Towanda** were built at the close of World War II, but there are still good sections of older highway to be found east of the interstate, between the newer four-lane and the railroad. The Carefree Motel and a Marathon Oil station are in Dwight, both dating from the 1930s. Near **Cayuga,** look for a photo opportunity to the west where, in a cluster of farm buildings, there is still a barnside ad for Meramec Caverns on Route 66 in Missouri.

From the early days of the old road, Meramec Caverns has been one of the most aggressive and colorful of all highway advertisers. And the cave is a great attraction still, so you may as well start thinking about a stop there. Besides, it's part of traveling to get excited, even to keep asking every few miles if we're *there* yet. You're a card-carrying adult now. You can even stick your feet out of the car window if you want to. Well, for a little while anyway . . . but leave your socks on.

Running a highway business is no easy task. And life can suddenly seem impossible when the highway department announces that the road will be moved. Some folks fold up and quit while others try to hang on. A few call up a special form of creativity born of desperation. Near **Pontiac** stands the Old Log Cabin Inn. Actually, it's a slightly newer version. The old inn fronted on the original Route 66 alignment next to the railroad. But the newer alignment of the highway was going to pass *behind* the place. Even the highway department pitched in and soon the problem was

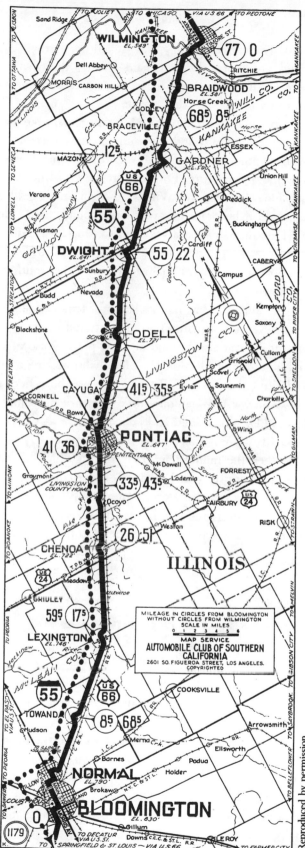

solved. The entire building was jacked up, turned around, and plopped down again—facing the new Route 66. If you're ready for a bite to eat, stop in. But save room for pie a little later on.

Continue south toward **Bloomington.** Like an old couple, **Normal** and Bloomington have sort of grown together. Both have universities and much Route 66 period architecture. Entering on the two-lane, zigzag along Pine, Linden, and Willow to Main Street. Follow Main until it becomes one-way northbound, then follow US 51 south, jogging via Oakland to Morris eastbound. Just before the business loop, turn right onto the service road, then right again following Beich south from town.

Bloomington has had its share of famous folks. Adlai Stevenson, a man who demonstrated that a political life can also be one of great public service, lived here. Major Gordon W. Lillie, who became a great Wild West show star as Pawnee Bill, was born here in 1866. And the now-famous surgeon Henry Braymore Blake, M.D., was reared and educated here as well. Colonel Blake was killed on a bright summer day in 1951 when the military air transport on which he was returning from duty in Korea was reportedly downed over the Sea of Japan. Despite pleas by Bloomington visitors, however, the city has yet to dedicate a memorial—or even a small parade—to honor him.

Bloomington to **S**t. **L**ouis

Heading south toward **McLean** on the west side of I-55, be sure to take time for a visit to Funk's Grove, just beyond **Shirley.** Turn west across the tracks for one of the more photogenic spots you'll find on this part of the route. Look over the old railway depot and the antique antique shop. Then head on across the road, and a little south, for the famous maple syrup plant. If you're planning to travel this way late in the year,

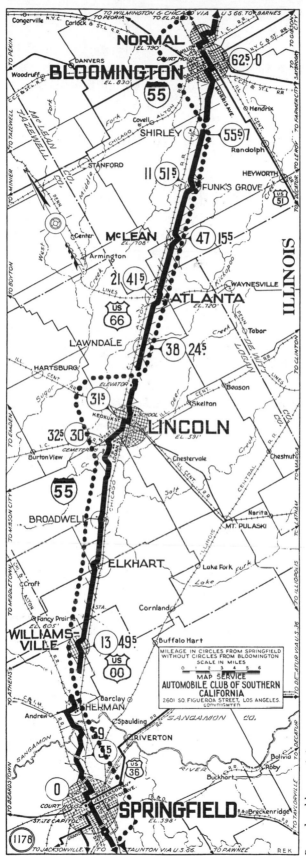

however, you'd best get your reservation in early. The
Funks have been making this syrup since the 1800s, so
they are quickly sold out. And take it from someone
who grew up in sugar bush country, this is *excellent*
maple syrup. What's more, you'll have a little bit of old
Route 66 right there in your refrigerator when you get
back home.

Getting hungry yet? Remember the room you
saved (or were supposed to save) for pie? Well, it's
almost on your plate. As a long-haul driver would say,
just keep the shiny side up and the muddy side down
as you head for the Dixie Truckers Home in McLean.
Built only a couple of years after Route 66 was
commissioned in 1926, the Dixie has since been a stop
of choice for many traveling this part of the highway.
And in all that time, the place has been closed only one
day. That was in 1965, when the original Dixie burned
down. Today, the Dixie still serves good food and great
pie. They also support the movement in Illinois to
revitalize old Route 66. What more could a roadie
want?

Leaving the Dixie, remember to keep the happy
side up and the chubby side down, following US 136
west for only a short distance. Watch for the old route
angling off to the south toward Atlanta. Continue on
and enter **Lincoln** via Business Loop 55. Follow
Kickapoo (recall Al Capp's famous Kickapoo Joy Juice?)
to the western jog on Keokuk to Logan, and then onto
5th, Washington, and Stringer. Lincoln is not a big
place, so it's fairly easy to get through town. If you
missed the Dixie, or feel the need for a coffee fix,
there's the [Dutch] Mill restaurant at Washington and
Stringer, in operation since 1931.

From this point to well beyond Springfield, this is
Lincoln Country. And indeed there are a number of
wonderful public attractions honoring the sixteenth
president. But there is also a commercial heaviness
about much of it. In fact, if you can find some place
where Lincoln is not advertised to have worked, stayed,
or stood, you might want to phone the Tourist Police
with an anonymous tip.

Continuing south, your stomach may tell you to
pass right on through **Broadwell,** but your nose and

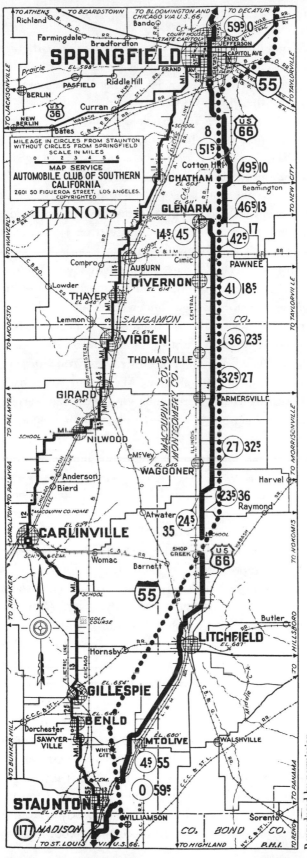

your mind may tell you otherwise as you near the Pig-Hip restaurant. In business along Route 66 since 1937, the place has a solid following among Illinois Route 66 fans. Try the Pig-Hip Special. And don't be afraid to ask for a roadie bag and maybe a Route 66 story to go with it. The Pig-Hip has plenty of each.

The four-lane is really the easier way through **Elkhart** and **Williamsville,** though there are sections of the old, old road along here, if you have the time to ferret them out. South of Williamsville, the old road ends and you must enter **Springfield** on I-55. Take the Sherman exit and follow the interstate business loop, which is mostly old Route 66, through town. There are scattered pieces of the old road around the city—one alignment even runs right under Lake Springfield. If the water level is low, the old roadbed is sometimes visible.

Heading south through Springfield on Business Loop 55, you'll have a choice of routes. You can jog west on South Grand and take MacArthur to Wabash to Chatham Road to Spaulding Orchard Road, turning south onto old SR 4. This is an old, old alignment of Route 66, dating from the 1920s, and if you are a true fan of mutant roadbeds, this is the alignment to follow. Although the road is laid out like a series of southerly jumps in a huge game of checkers, the accompanying map is quite consistent with the route through **Virden** and **Carlinville** to **Staunton.**

If you find roadside remnants of Route 66 from the 1930s more interesting, continue on Business Loop 55 and take the Chatham exit. Follow old Route 66 on the west side of the interstate south toward **Glenarm,** where you might get a shot of culture at Mort's Roadhouse. The building itself dates from 1893 and for most of its life has been a garage—which may account for part of its attraction to the biker set. It's vintage Route 66. So be a sport . . . but bring your own leather. Continue south to the dead end, then cross to the east side of I-55, and turn south again through **Litchfield** and **Mt. Olive.** Litchfield is home to the Ariston Cafe, another Route 66 original.

Recross I-55 opposite Staunton to connect with SR 4 and remain on the west side to pick up SR 157. If you're passing through **Hamel** at dusk or during the

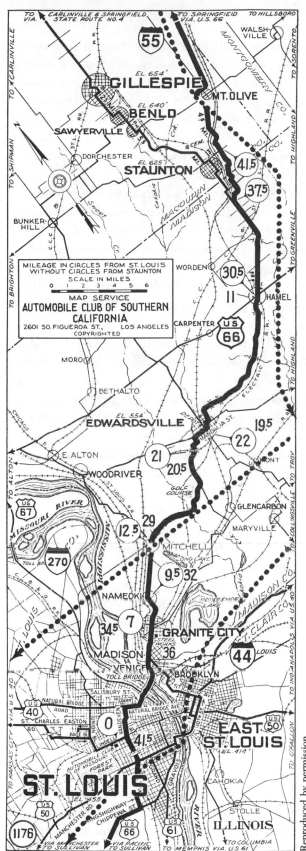

night, a neon cross on a church there helps speed you
safely on your way. It's blue and it's big, but most
travelers get an oddly warm feeling from the cross.
Even though it is done in neon, there is something
tasteful about it—unlike some of the rotating beacons
in Los Angeles, which make their churches look more
like some place to buy fried chicken. No, this cross is
not like that, especially in the rain. It was placed
on the front of St. Paul's Lutheran Church by the
Brunnworths, whose son, Oscar, had been drowned
during the invasion of Italy at Anzio in World War II.
Clearly advertising nothing, the cross is simply a
comforting tribute.

Follow SR 157 south through **Edwardsville** to
the junction with Chain of Rocks Road, just north of
I-270. Here, you will have a choice about which route
to follow. If you are already familiar with St. Louis or
are short on time, you may wish to skirt the city on
I-270, rejoining the old road on the west side. Of the
old alignments followed by Route 66 across the
Mississippi River, only the McKinley Bridge still carries
traffic.

However, you may want to take a stroll out onto
Chain of Rocks Bridge, begun in 1927 and in service
until the 1960s. It is one of the few bridges in the
world with a radical bend in the middle.

The bridge is in superb condition and well worth
a look. From SR 157, take Chain of Rocks Road west
beyond **Mitchell.** At the SR 203 junction, cross to the
south side of I-270 and follow Chain of Rocks Road.
Continue west over the canal bridge to the end of the
two-lane at a dirt-and-tire barrier. The entrance to
Chain of Rocks Bridge is just beyond.

Parking can be a problem, but a walk out onto the
bridge is a worthwhile experience. Chain of Rocks was
repaved for its part in John Carpenter's 1981 film *Escape
from New York.* It was, in fact, the bridge over which
patch-eyed Kurt Russell made good his escape and upon
which Adrienne Barbeau breathed her bosomy last.

If you've decided to take the northern beltline
route around St. Louis, return to westbound I-270. To
make the McKinley Bridge crossing from **Venice,** take
SR 203 south from Mitchell. Continue through **Granite**

City and take Nameoki Road (SR 203) to Madison Avenue, which becomes Broadway Avenue in Venice, and then straight across 4th Street and onto the bridge. The McKinley Bridge has been in service for eighty years, so you might expect its deck surface to be in very poor shape, and it is. This route through the Venice area also requires caution. It's not a place to have a flat, run out of fuel, or ask questions.

CHAPTER

2

Missouri

Most place-names suffer when they are translated from a mother tongue and later contracted. But not *Aux Arc,* the name of an early Missouri trading post. In the original French, the term is plain, sensible. Like shoes with laces. Yet in its modern form, *Ozark* becomes a mythic word. A mystery. Not dark or ominous but a whisper-word full of timeless secrets. The Ozarks. A place of independent people with soft smiles and stout, natural reserve—backbone of the Show Me State.

Missourians, hands thrust securely into their pockets, can stand for an hour while they wait for you to state your case, make your best offer, or ask directions. In the end, they'll know all they need to about your business and you'll know nothing more about them than you did an hour ago. Some say that comes naturally to folks of solid mining-farming-mountain stock who had to contend with riverboat gamblers, Damn-Yankees, Kansas guerrillas, and the weather hereabouts. Others say plainly that the Missouri attitude comes from too much time spent talking to mules—which can teach great patience but little in the art of light conversation.

But don't take that to mean that people from Missouri are humorless, for they are not that at all. What other state, with heavy interests in manufacturing, shipping, and the aerospace industry, declares with a straight face that it is also a world leader in the production of corncob pipes? Where else would you find a county government so fed up with the North-South quarrel over slavery that it refused to stand with either faction and instead formed the completely independent Kingdom of Callaway? And along what other stretch of old Route 66 would you be likely to see a hand-lettered sign advertising GUN & DOG SWAP MEET—WOMEN OK (MAYBE)? Not tongue-in-cheek humor exactly, but sly. Very sly.

The larger part of Missouri hangs suspended between its two major cities, St. Louis and Kansas City. Both these cities have dithered over the years, each feeling at various times inferior, each courting greatness, yet often shrinking from the self-surgery that greatness sometimes requires. Through this try-and-try-again atmosphere, old Route 66 plunges diagonally across the state, following the course of the Osage Trail, Kickapoo Trace and, later, the Federal Wire Road, south and west toward Kansas and Oklahoma.

Perhaps more than any other state through which Route 66 passes, Missouri is a region of great contrast. Something of the spirit of *Tom Sawyer* and *The Shepherd of the Hills* is still present here, along with the torment of civil and border wars. Yet there is also a lingering sense of willing endurance handed down from Pony Express riders and the redoubtable Lindbergh.

At a loss for ways to represent the land and culture and people in a single slogan for tourists, the state department of tourism finally surrendered. "Come to Missouri," they finally wrote. "There's no state quite like it." True enough.

If tree-shaded main streets full of memories of old Route 66 are your interest, if you are an antiquer and

general poker-about, or if you simply want to cruise
smoothly through the roller-coaster hills, be sure to
take a little extra time for Missouri. There *is* no other
place quite like it.

St. Louis to Waynesville

Old Route 66 alignments through **St. Louis** are
plentiful but serpentine. So unless you have time to
backtrack several times across the city, it's best to take
a hybrid route made up of alignments from several
periods.

If you have chosen to skirt the city on I-270 to
the north, you'll still be following an alignment from
the 1930s through the '50s. Old Route 66 lies directly
beneath I-270 from Riverview Drive to Lindbergh
Boulevard. At Lindbergh (US 67), Route 66 turned
south to pass through **Kirkwood** to [New] Watson
Road. The traffic is not heavy over this section except
during rush hours and Kirkwood is a charming
community with much of the feeling of an earlier time
preserved. Look for the railroad depot, a classic and still
in service.

And if you've an eye for trains and steam
locomotives, there are some splendid displays at the
National Museum of Transport, just a few minutes
away. The museum is a mile or so west of I-270, on
Barrett Station Road between Dougherty Ferry Road
and Big Bend Road.

Dating from the late 1800s to the final days of
steam after World War II, the motive power here
ranges from early pufferbellies to the giant Santa Fe
2-10-4, which once offered Route 66 travelers the
chance to race with a truly fast freight, highballing
through the West ("Faster, Daddy, faster . . .") where
the old road runs right alongside Santa Fe's rifle-shot
tracks. There are lots of other exhibits, too, but the
great iron horses still steal the show.

Following your visit, continue northwest on

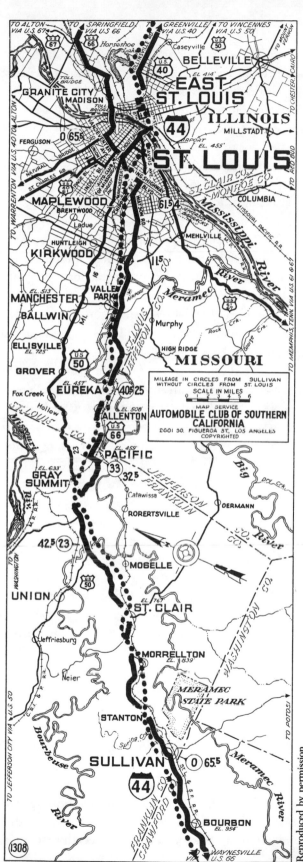

Barrett and turn west on Manchester. Very little of
Watson Road and the old Route 66 establishments still
exists west of Kirkwood Road. So the far more
interesting alignment from the 1920s and '30s is
Manchester Road, which can be followed west to **Gray
Summit.**

If you plan on taking a through-town route, the
McKinley Bridge crossing leads via Salisbury Street to
an old business loop. For a total-tourist side trip,
connect with I-70 southbound and exit shortly for the
Jefferson National Expansion Memorial and Gateway
Arch, co-located with several excellent museums,
historic buildings, and riverfront attractions. Elegant
Eads Bridge, the world's first steel-truss span, is also
just to the north. And if you are willing to forgo a
couple of hours' sleep, you'll find the bridge especially
beautiful in early morning light.

For a convenient route from the park, rejoin the
old alignment via Chouteau Avenue just a few blocks to
the south and turn west. Continue past Checkerboard
Square (Were you a Tom Mix radio fan? Can you still
sing the Ralston Straight Shooter's theme song?) and
turn south again on Tucker (formerly 12th Street),
which becomes Gravois Avenue. At Chippewa Street
(SR 366), turn west and continue as Chippewa becomes
Watson Road.

If you are screaming-for-ice-cream, be sure to stop
at Ted Drewes' Frozen Custard. It'll put love in your
tummy and most of the flavors will look fine on your
clothes, too. The Coral Court Motel, world famous for
its art deco design—it's on the National Register—and
locally famous as a most discreet sin-at-noon palace, is
also along this stretch of old Route 66.

From Kirkwood Road, Watson Road simply
disappears under I-44, so turn north on Kirkwood and
west again on Manchester Road, which was Route 66
before a newer version of Watson Road was completed
in 1932. Or, if you prefer, you can continue on I-44 to
the Six Flags exit and follow the business loop to **Gray
Summit.** The interstate route is not totally without
redemption. At the **Eureka** exit, on the north service
road at the overpass, is Phil's Bar-B-Cue, one of the
few places of its kind to serve up a good breakfast as

well as pizza, a mess of catfish, and ribs. Further west, in **Pacific,** is the Red Cedar Inn. Completed in 1934, the inn is a landmark of old Route 66 and has recently reopened under the same family's careful management.

On Manchester Road, as you roll through the lovely Missouri countryside, imagine how all this must have been back in 1926, because this section remains much as it was over sixty years ago. Virtually no maps existed back then, and the few available travel guides reminded drivers to close each farm gate behind them, since part of the roadway still crossed private property.

Continue through Gray Summit and cross over I-44 to the southwest, bear west, recross the interstate, and then follow County AT southwest as it parallels I-44. **Villa Ridge** was once a very big deal along the old highway. And The Diamonds—"world's largest roadside restaurant," according to its owner, Spencer Groff—was once the main attraction here. In the 1920s, he'd run some tiny, but highly successful businesses here. One was an all-night banana stand. Undoubtedly a first in itself. One good thing led to another, however, and Groff put up a building in the shape of a baseball diamond. That's how The Diamonds, a place that served up to a million travelers a year, got its name. The original is now a truck stop and the business Spencer Groff started has moved a couple of miles east. But there's enough of the old feeling up here to go around.

West of Villa Ridge, old Route 66 continues west as North Outer Road to County AH, crossing I-44 to the south side. Continue on South Outer Road and SR 47. At **St. Clair,** recross I-44 to the north side on SR 30 and continue on County WW until it heads north, then continue on North Outer Road to   are you ready yet?—**Stanton,** Missouri. Home of . . . ? That's right, the world-famous Meramec Caverns and alleged hideout of rascally Jesse James and his gang.

One of the best-remembered places along the old highway, Meramec Caverns was opened for the tourist business in 1935 by champion roadside entrepreneur Lester Dill. Some locals still say that if Dill had not discovered the caverns, he'd have dug them himself. That's a fair assessment, because Lester B. Dill probably

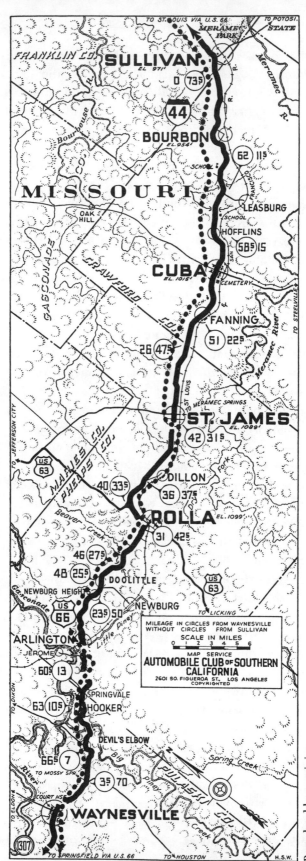

MILEAGE IN CIRCLES FROM WAYNESVILLE
WITHOUT CIRCLES FROM SULLIVAN

SCALE IN MILES
0 1 2 3 4 5 6

MAP SERVICE
AUTOMOBILE CLUB OF SOUTHERN
CALIFORNIA
2601 SO. FIGUEROA ST.   LOS ANGELES
COPYRIGHTED

did invent that great American institution—the bumper sticker. So do make time for this attraction. Much of the copy recited by the tour guides hasn't changed since the 1930s. And if you don't happen to know who Kate Smith was, this is as good a place as any to find out.

Crossing to the south side at Stanton at the junction of County JJ and County W, continue west on South Outer Road. In **Sullivan,** keep an eye out for the grand old Shamrock Motel structure. Then continue on the south side through **Bourbon,** where the main street is Old Highway 66. Actually, the name Bourbon is something of a misnomer since this is wine country.

If you missed Meramec Caverns or are a closet spelunker, Onondaga Cave, another old Route 66 attraction, is just south of **Leasburg.** In **Cuba,** be sure to take notice of or stay at the Wagon Wheel Motel. It's well kept and vintage Americana. All it lacks is one of those mirrored globes on a pedestal out front to go with the elves. By now, it may even have one of those.

From Cuba, continue on County ZZ and KK into **St. James.** This area, **Rosati** especially, is known for its table grapes. If that strikes an appetite chord, plan to stop at one of the little grape stands along old Route 66. Only a few of the older stands remain, and there is a move afoot by the Missouri Department of Transportation to close even the last of these tiny stands down. It seems that people still like to stop, and now that the interstate makes it so difficult to get to the old road, folks just pull to the side of I-44 and visit the stands on foot. Yes sir, sure does sound like it's the grape stands' fault, doesn't it?

Just beyond St. James, there is a break in the old route, so rejoin I-44 or cross to the north side via SR 8 and 68 and continue. At **Rolla,** the easier route to follow is Business Loop 44, which was a late alignment of old Route 66. Leaving town, follow Martin Spring Drive, which doubles as the south-side service road, and continue on to **Doolittle** (established near **Centerville**).

The town was named for former air-race winner Jimmy Doolittle, who once bolstered sagging morale in the United States by coaxing a tiny flight of sixteen standard-issue army B-25 bombers off the pitching deck

of the USS *Hornet* for a raid on Tokyo, just a few
months after the attack on Pearl Harbor. It wasn't a
mighty blow, but it was a good sharp thumb in the eye
at a time when not much was going right for us. As
you drive down Doolittle's main street today, say a little
word of thanks that guys like Jimmy are around when
they're needed.

Approaching **Arlington,** it's necessary to take
I-44 for a short distance. For a real old-road treat,
however, exit at County J southbound and continue
west on County Z. Then turn south at the first
opportunity before Big Piney River. You're now right in
the crook of Devils Elbow, a section of highway famous
among Route 66 roadies for its river-bluff scenery and a
lovely old steel-truss bridge built in 1923. There's no
traffic on this loop, so take time for a stroll and perhaps
a picnic lunch. Continue west to return to the County
Z four-lane and roll on toward **St. Robert.**

Cross to the north at the junction with Business
Loop 44 and continue into **Waynesville.** There is
some interesting, sometimes Romanesque, architecture
here, plus a favorite local hangout, The Tinkle Bar.
Things are very straightforward in Waynesville.

Waynesville to Joplin

From Waynesville, follow SR 17 south across the
interstate and through **Laquey.** Where SR 17 heads
south, follow County AB west into **Hazelgreen.**
Continue on the south-side frontage road toward
Sleeper, cross to the north side at County F, and
follow the north frontage road into **Lebanon.**

Joining County W, you will find a fairly long run
that gets well away from the interstate almost all the
way into **Springfield**—and it's a beautiful drive
through unspoiled farmland and small communities. At
Phillipsburg, cross I-44 to the south and follow

County CC and OO through **Marshfield** and past
Buena Vista's Exotic Animal Paradise, a ranch-sized
spread of wild animals and rare birds. From **Strafford,**
continue on OO (SR 744), which becomes Kearney
Street in Springfield.

Springfield—"Queen City of the Ozarks"—is
worth a browse, especially if you're doing a little
photography or are interested in period architecture.
From Kearney, turn south on Glenstone Avenue,
then west onto St. Louis and College Streets. After
a few blocks, you'll notice the Shrine Mosque, a local
wonder and an old Route 66 landmark. If you can
imagine the Grand Old Opry in Nashville (or your old
grammar school) as it might have been designed by an
itinerant Arab architect, you'll have a pretty good image
of the mosque. It's wonderful, and in its day hosted
some of the biggest acts around.

Farther west, you'll also pass the old calaboose on
Central Square, near where Wild Bill Hickok killed
Dave Tutt in one of those provoked shoot-outs for
which the American West is so famous. As this story
goes, Hickok had lost heavily to Tutt in a poker game.
To buy time (literally), Hickok had given his pocket
watch to Tutt to hold, with the express understanding
that the watch would not be seen in public. Too
embarrassing to Hickok, you see. But Tutt wore it
anyway, Hickok killed him outright—there are plaques
in the square to mark where each stood—and everyone
settled down to watch Hickok's trial. The verdict was
self-defense. But no one seemed to notice that, with
Tutt now dead, Hickok had his watch back and no
longer owed anything on his gambling debt.

Heading on out of town on the Chestnut
Expressway, you may ponder such matters. You also
might give some thought to the old stories about how
Ozark folk have often been accused of poor bloodlines
due to excessive intermarriage. And that might even
have been partially true at one time. But consider this:
Springfield represents the gene pool that produced
none other than Kathleen Turner. With her now-
unchallenged acting ability, her smouldering try-it-if-
you-dare sexuality, and her down-home beauty, the rest
of the country would do well to look into the records

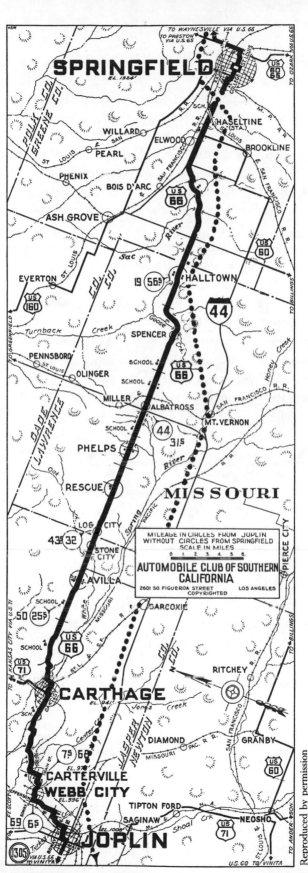

SPRINGFIELD
EL. 1324'

POLK CO.
GREENE CO.

TO WAYNESVILLE VIA U.S. 66
TO PRESTON VIA U.S. 65

US 60-65

TO OZARK VIA U.S. 65

WILLARD
PEARL
ELWOOD
SAN

PHENIX
BOIS D'ARC

HASELTINE (STA.)
BROOKLINE

M. P. R. R.

US 66

ASH GROVE

US 60

EVERTON
US 160

19 56⁹ HALLTOWN

44

Sac River

TO BILLINGS

GREENFIELD

Turnback Creek
PENNSBORO
OLINGER
ST.LOUIS

SPENCER

Goose Ck.

US 66

Honey Creek

SCHOOL
MILLER
ALBATROSS
SCHOOL
PHELPS
MT. VERNON
44
3¹⁵
River

SAN FRANCISCO R. R.

DADE CO.
LAWRENCE CO.

RESCUE

MISSOURI

Oak Ck.

LOG CITY
43⁵ 32
STONE CITY
AVILLA

Spring River

Pacific

PIERCE CITY

MILEAGE IN CIRCLES FROM JOPLIN
WITHOUT CIRCLES FROM SPRINGFIELD
SCALE IN MILES
0 1 2 3 4 5 6
AUTOMOBILE CLUB OF SOUTHERN
CALIFORNIA
2601 SO. FIGUEROA STREET   LOS ANGELES
COPYRIGHTED

SCHOOL
50 25⁹
US 66
White River
Missouri
SCHOOL

SARCOXIE

TO KANSAS CITY VIA U.S. 71
US 71

CARTHAGE
EL. 941'

RITCHEY

TO BILLINGS

Jones Creek

DIAMOND
Missouri Pac. R. R.
GRANBY
US 60

7⁵ 6⁹
CARTERVILLE
WEBB CITY
EL. 996'

TIPTON FORD
SAGINAW
Shoal Crk.
NEOSHO
US 71

TO ANDERSON

69 6⁵

1305
VIA U.S. 66
TO VINITA

JOPLIN

U.S. 60 TO VINITA

JASPER CO.
NEWTON CO.

here. As genetic codes go, Springfield has a line that is unbeatable.

The section of old Route 66 from Springfield west is a real treat. From **Halltown**—an interesting stop for antiquers—continue west through **Paris Springs Junction** for a cruise on old, old Route 66, rather than jogging south onto SR 96. At the junction with County N, cross to the south of SR 96. Turn west from County N at the first intersection and cross the old steel-truss bridge. Continue through Casey's Corner at what was once Spencer, cross to the north of SR 96 at the stop, and continue toward **Carthage.**

The town names along this stretch of Route 66 sing a special song in passing: **Albatross**, **Phelps**, **Rescue . . . Log City** and **Stone City** are only shadows of what they were. But **Avilla** survives, and some of the country schools shown on the accompanying map are still here. Much of the rest— tiny resorts and small businesses that grew with the wonder of old Route 66—have fallen into ruin.

Indeed, from this section of the old route on west, through parts of Oklahoma, Texas, New Mexico, and Arizona, the number of abandoned businesses and highway attractions increases greatly. In some ways, that's a sad fact. But there is a more cheerful view, championed by observers like John Brinkerhoff Jackson, that there is a great need for relics like these.

Since we can only experience history through our imaginations, they suggest, the ruins we encounter serve as vital props for any journey of the mind in time. In viewing some roadside ruin, then, we are better able to re-create for ourselves the period in which it stood. An interesting thought—that by seeing clearly what remains, each of us gives some ruin a second life. A chance to exist again, as it once was, in the projection of our mind's eye.

Just knowing this can make the traveling more passionate, the seeing more profound, as you make your way along this old road—which is itself a relic. Yet a relic that you may revive, if only for a moment, by your passing.

Carthage is next and it, too, is special. A businesslike county seat, it is peopled with individualists of the first rank—the notorious Belle Starr was born here. There is also a strong, creative thread in Carthage that seems to go way back. Still following SR 96, take at least a moment for the town square and the classic Jasper County Courthouse. The clock has been reinstalled after taking the cure for striking thirteen too often. And the courthouse lawn looks pretty good, too. Remember the Missouri sense of humor? Carthage does. Some years back, when the lawn was redone, someone slipped turnip seed into the replanting mixture. The grass was only mediocre, but it was a bumper turnip crop for embarrassed officials.

Route 66 continues on through Carthage to the US 71 junction west of town. Follow US 71 south to the Carterville exit, following Main Street through the S-curve in **Carterville** and onto Broadway in **Web City**. If you have a hankering for a chocolate soda and a comic book about now, try the restored Bradbury-Bishop Drugstore just a block off the old route at Main and Daugherty Streets. Then, heading for **Joplin,** follow Madison (US 71) south.

Lying at the edge of an ore-producing region stretching along old Route 66 through Kansas and into Oklahoma, peaceful Joplin sits atop countless abandoned mining tunnels and a rough history—beginning with a two-town rivalry. A local judge and his friend, a Methodist minister named Joplin, had settled a nice, lead-rich town, when a competing town called Murphysburg sprang up just across Turkey Creek.

The judge got himself all riled up about that, and the other town's developer, Murphy, got counterriled. Soon someone brought in a bushwhacker called Three-Fingered Pete. Then, someone else hired a brawler called Reckless Bill, and everybody began having at it on a regular basis. Mining got all mixed up with religion, which got all mixed up with the law and the egos of both towns. In the end, it became such an awful mess that the state legislature stepped in, Siamesed the two towns under the single name City of Joplin, and told everyone to behave themselves or they wouldn't get a railroad.

So things settled down quickly and the miners returned to their labors all along this old section of the route. In fact, they worked so hard and long that the road itself developed a habit of falling into abandoned tunnels. Several detours have been necessary since a cave-in of the road in 1939. And as this is being written, there's a new detour at **Galena,** just down the highway. So, drive softly—and when you walk, don't stamp your feet. You might fall right on through to Tiananmen Square.

The easier route through Joplin follows US 71 to SR 66 west. If you want to linger along the old route in Missouri, try Dixie Lee's Dine and Dance Bar at the west end of town. Along with Dutch's Top Hat and Dana's Bo Peep, Dixie Lee's was a last-chance saloon during the time Kansas was dry. And while some of the bloom is off this surviving roadside rose, you can still check out the local high life and brush up early on your Texas two-step.

West of Joplin, watch for a sign: OLD ROUTE 66 NEXT RIGHT. The newer SR 66 alignment continues on to Kansas, but a turn here will put you on another rare, surviving section of the original route. There's a nice resurrected feeling about these few miles, which have somehow found protection through local use.

CHAPTER

3

Kansas

There are only a dozen miles of old Route 66 in Kansas. But they are part of a saw-toothed run from Joplin, Missouri, to Vinita, Oklahoma, that's truly a crackerjack stretch of highway and history. If you've ever wondered why all the old-timers seem to have huge, nautical compasses mounted in their cars or camper cabs, one look at the map for this part of old Route 66 will provide the answer. When you're on a road that zigzags along section lines rather than following a more direct course, it's only easy to guess your direction when it's early or late in the day. The rest of the time you'd better have some other means of knowing which way you're headed.

All of which fits with the old Middle American tradition of never admitting that you don't know something. Most people who grew up from Ohio to Oklahoma know not to ask directions of strangers or service station attendants. Instead of saying that they don't know (when they don't), well-intentioned midwesterners will just give you the most plausible answer they can think of. And it rarely has anything to do with accuracy.

There are a couple of other things to remember as you roll from southern Missouri on into Kansas and Oklahoma. The first is that this area is pretty close to the buckle on the Bible Belt, so you'd best save any snappy ecumenical jokes you have for later. The other thing is to think twice before ordering Italian in these parts. Oklahomans, for example, take their religion and the way their meat is cooked pretty seriously. There are more churches and barbecue joints between the Kansas border and Oklahoma City than some people see in a lifetime. On other matters, excepting football perhaps, Oklahomans are far more laid back.

It's a little different just the other side of the line. In Kansas, they tend to take *everything* seriously. It's not a place to cut up much. Especially in a restaurant at Sunday brunch.

Some of this traces right back to the kind of righteous single-mindedness with which issues have been settled here. People who got caught in the sweeping crossfire between Quantrill's Raiders and the Jayhawkers, during the Civil War period, quickly learned that most everything about life could get serious in a hurry. Later, as the labor movement was beginning in the zinc and lead mines of this region, both the company goons and militant union members took the matter right into the streets. There were times during the mid-1930s when old Route 66 itself ran red, usually with the blood of determined strikers. This is country that has been cleared, farmed, and mined the hard way. And parents have taught their children well.

But a hundred years of conflict in this little corner of Kansas has produced something of great value to the traveler as well. The people here, along the old road, are as clear and honest and forthcoming as can be found anywhere. What's more, they have a sense of history and a knowledge of themselves which sets them apart.

No one dawdles much here. Work still comes before much else. Of all the states through which old Route 66 passed, Kansas was among the first to see that the highway was properly paved in concrete. The towns here—Galena, Riverton, Baxter Springs—are also among the quietest and most serene you'll find. Take a stroll down by one of the rivers. Walk along a neighborhood street. Listen to the crickets and the screen doors. There are only a few miles of Kansas on the old route, but this place is a big part of the true America we all carry somewhere in our hearts.

It's no wonder Dorothy was so happy to be home again.

Galena to **B**axter **S**prings

Continuing on the older alignment through **Galena,** turn south on Main Street. Long before Prohibition, when the mining boom could still be heard, this was called Red Hot Street in Galena. And it was that, no doubt about it. The saloons and bawdy houses stayed open twenty-four hours a day, keeping the miners picked clean from payday to payday.

In the beginning, the town of Empire had richer mines than Galena. So, to prevent unwelcome Galenans from making a daily beeline for the better diggings, the protective folks of Empire built a high fence of timbers along the town's border. Galena waited some months until the entire fence was completed, then simply burned it to the ground—so much for the stockade concept. Later, when the mines in Empire began to play out, Galena annexed the town. Departing Galena-Empire, continue on SR 66.

Even if you have only a mild bridge fetish, the Kansas portion of old Route 66 will leave an impression. There are a couple of rainbow-style concrete-truss bridges near **Baxter Springs**—one generously supplied with youthful graffiti. Names don't exactly go up in lights around here, but at least one bridge seems to be a marquee for locally sown wild oats. To check the roster as well as follow the old road,

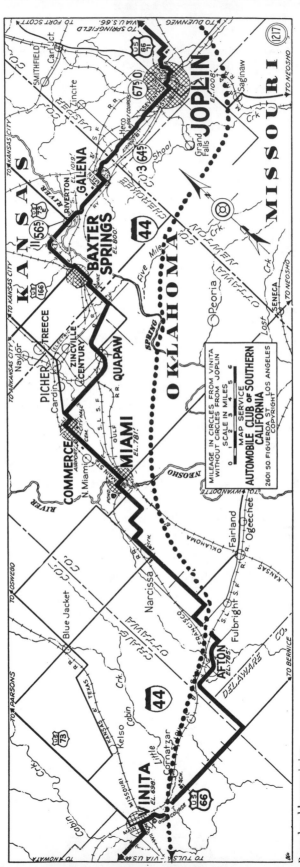

take the alignment that heads west along a line of aging telephone poles just south of **Riverton.**

Both Galena and Baxter Springs are working hard to keep their heritage fresh and their association with old Route 66 alive. There are excellent museums in both towns. And to help make the transition from Midwest to West, make a stop at Murphey's Restaurant in Baxter Springs. Originally a bank, the building played unwilling host to one Jesse James who strolled in empty-handed, on a fine May day, and strolled out with almost $3,000. Today, the spot offers a nice chance to grab a cup of java and a little off-the-road relaxation. Some say, though, that the ghost of Tom Howard still hangs about in places like this. So, if someone behind you tells you quietly to raise 'em, don't turn around . . .

CHAPTER

4

Oklahoma

When you talk about outlaws in Oklahoma, it's important to distinguish between regular outlaws and elected outlaws. The state has certainly had more than its share of both. First came all the sod-busters who jumped the line early during the great Land Rush. They undoubtedly set the trend for everybody. Later, when some political hustlers decided that Oklahoma City would make a more profitable center for state government, they simply stole the Great Seal from the existing capitol in Guthrie and hauled it on down to its present site.

One result is that good outlawing became something of a fifth estate in Oklahoma.

Like many of the better class of outlaws, Jesse James and his pals started out in Missouri, but spent a lot of time in these parts. So did Pretty Boy Floyd, an Oklahoman from age five, who soon became a Robin Hood of the 1930s. An expert in the bank-robbing business, Pretty Boy always found time to tear up whatever farm mortgages he could find around a bank. And when on the lam, it is said that he would pay poor farm families for a meal—and silence, of course—with a $1,000 bill.

All across the state, Depression-ridden people understood his motives and were cheered by his exploits. So they defended Pretty Boy and cared for him as their own. When the hapless Floyd was finally gunned down by the FBI, twenty thousand mourners turned out for his burial. It was the biggest funeral Oklahoma has ever seen. As for Ma Barker and her sons, together with Bonnie Parker, Clyde Barrow, Machine Gun Kelly, and the rest of the outlaws-turned-killers, good riddance. No folk songs are sung about them. None need be.

For many Route 66 travelers, Oklahoma has often been no more than a place to be driven through quickly in order to get to the good stuff farther west. Too bad for them. Because Oklahoma, once truly seen and fully experienced, is one of the most beautiful—and most openhanded—places to be found anywhere. Cyclists and hikers could do no better than pedal or hoof their way through the gently rolling country from the Kansas border to Oklahoma City.

In the western reaches of the state the land is even more beautiful, lying rumpled in all directions like a giant designer bedsheet, small farms and friendly towns among the creases. More attractive to automobile drivers or motorcyclists than to ten-speed riders, perhaps, but magnificent nonetheless.

For real pit-barbecue freaks, however, the entire state is a groaning board. Closet cases of smoke fever may be forced out into the open, and all but the most devout vegetarians will be sorely tested. So you may as well learn the tune: Get your ribs on Route 66.

The remarkable thing is that in Oklahoma as nowhere else, art and architecture go hand in hand with folk history, down-home hospitality, and the sweetness of the green-on-red land. Truly the birthplace of old Route 66, Oklahoma is well worth knowing. Take some time here. Let the people of Oklahoma get to know you, too.

Quapaw to **O**klahoma **C**ity

Nearly all of old Route 66 has been preserved and
remains in daily use throughout eastern Oklahoma.
Since the interstate turnpike is a toll road here, most
local and regional travel is done on the Free Road—old
Route 66. And an excellent highway it is, too. You'll
have little difficulty following this unbroken 260-mile
section of the old road as it meanders along from the
Kansas border to Oklahoma City.

From Baxter Springs, follow US 69 south into
Quapaw. If it's coming on nighttime, you may be able
to do a little ghost-busting here. For one and a half
miles east of Quapaw, on a bluff called Devil's
Promenade near the Spring River, is the home of
Spooklight, an apparition that sometimes drew as many
as a thousand cars per night during the peak spook
season. Spooklight (no joke here) appears as a dancing,
bobbing, rolling ball of light, seen in these parts
regularly for years. Sometimes Spooklight has even been
seen entering parked cars.

There are lots of theories, but thus far nothing
approaching an adequate explanation. Scientists and
army technicians of nearly every stripe have tested this
and that, but to no avail. One of the better technical
theories is that Spooklight is really only a wandering,
atmospheric refraction of headlights on the nearby
highway. But that falls a little short when it is recalled
that Spooklight was first seen by the Quapaw Indians in
the mid-1800s. Not exactly a lot of cars around back
then. Undaunted by a lack of theoretical structure,
Spookie just keeps on hanging out here. To nearly
everyone's delight.

Unless you're spooked, follow US 69 south then
west from Quapaw and jog through **Commerce,** home
of Mickey (the Commerce Comet) Mantle. Entering
town southbound, jog west on Commerce and south
again on Main Street, heading on down to **Miami**
(pronounced *My-am-uh*).

Continue through Miami on Main Street, and if

possible, take time for a look at the Coleman Theater. Much of the interior has already been restored and Miami is raising funds to buy back the Wurlitzer organ that was once the theater's centerpiece.

From Miami, follow US 69 through **Narcissa,** join US 60, then cross under the turnpike, and continue to **Afton.** Because so much tourist business has been lost to through traffic on the interstate, only a few attractions have remained open. The Buffalo Ranch is one of them. A petting zoo, barbecue, and buffalo, too. What more could the imagination desire? A llama or a yak? They've got 'em and it's worth a stop.

In Afton, an interesting spot for collectors of nearly any ilk is the saddle shop, across the street and just east of the old Palmer Hotel. Here you'll find a whole wall of matchbooks, some dating back fifty years or so. None are for sale, but that can't stop you from making a bid on the wall itself.

From Afton, continue south, then west on US 60. **Vinita** is next, named for Vinnie Ream, the sculptress whose rendering of Abraham Lincoln now stands in the nation's capital. Through Vinita, follow US 60 to the junction with SR 66 just before **White Oak.** Then continue southwest on the Free Road into **Chelsea,** the very first oil-patch town and one of the few to have a perfectly preserved example of a Sears mail-order house. It is a private residence, however, so take care not to disturb if you stop by for a look.

Farther south, the village of **Bushyhead** is gone now. But **Foyil** is snug enough, with a nice loop of old, old Route 66, in its original pink concrete, curving through town. Even more interesting is Galloway's Totem Pole Park, a few miles east on SR 28A, where you can see the results of that rare flash of artistic genius some roadside entrepreneurs find in themselves. Take along plenty of film, though. The place is a challenge to portray.

On down the road, **Claremore** is worth some extra time for a visit to the Will Rogers Memorial. Claremore is also the hometown of Lynn Riggs, author of *Green Grow the Lilacs,* on which the Pulitzer Prize– winning *Oklahoma!* is based. Entering town, angle west at the first signal and continue parallel to SR 66 on

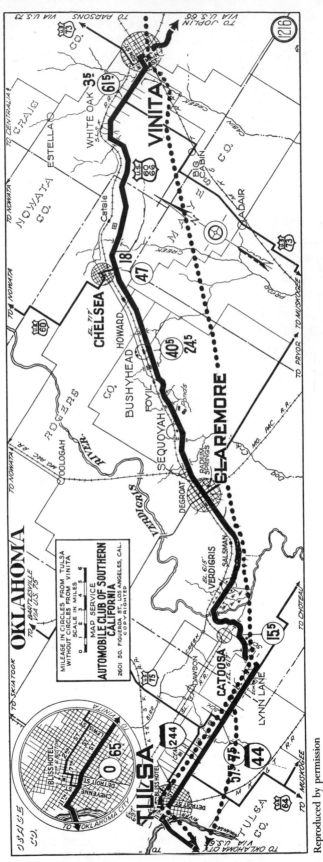

Reproduced by permission

J. M. Davis Boulevard. This is the old route and motel
row in Claremore. The Claremore Motor Inn, though
not a real landmark, is comfortable and a good place to
collect road stories from the former highway patrolman
at the desk. Also, keep a nose-scan going for The Pits.
It's on the left and one of the better barbecue places
around. Also, if time permits, check out the Davis Gun
Museum. Even people who don't like guns are often
impressed, and it is a whale of a collection.

Continue southwest, rejoining the Free Road.
About ten miles beyond town, you'll cross Spunky
Creek. There was even a Fort Spunky here at one time,
and though the name sounds a bit like *Lassie Joins F
Troop,* this was once very wild territory. It took spunk
to live around here very long.

Just a few miles farther, after the highway bends
west, watch for the nonidentical twin spans over the
Verdigris River. Most everyone feels compelled to
photograph this odd couple of bridges—some locals
even call them Felix and Oscar—and more than a few
travelers are bothered by the difference. But, then, who
would notice these structures at all if they matched?

Beyond the Verdigris, watch for the old Blue
Whale Amusement Park on the right. It's little more
than a photo opportunity now, but who knows?
Catoosa has grit as well as a name derived from a
Cherokee expression referring to People of the Light.
It's not clear, though, if the Cherokees were seeing the
same kind of light as the Quapaws.

Nearing **Tulsa,** the Free Road sometimes gets a
little crowded, so keep a sharp eye out for the SR 167
junction.

Tulsa has lots of visual and gastronomic interest
along old Route 66, so plan to take the city route if
possible. Otherwise, enter I-44 and continue until
Sapulpa. If you'll be touring Tulsa, take 193rd Avenue
(SR 167) south and turn west again on 11th Street.
Admiral Place is an alternative alignment but less
interesting overall. Watch for the Metro Diner, just past
the stadium at Tulsa University. A little farther on,
there's the Route 66 Diner, a bit west of the big Bama
Pies building on the north side. Both are fairly new
restaurants and are already becoming landmarks for

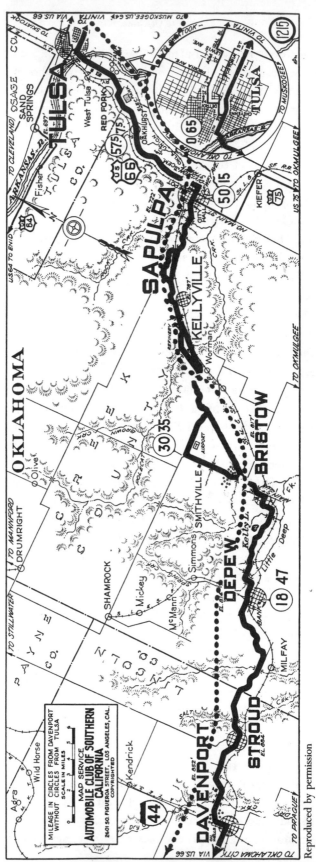

Reproduced by permission

Route 66 travelers. Continuing west on 11th Street, notice the old Warehouse Market, a marvelous piece of Art Deco and a possible center for neighborhood restoration and redevelopment.

Just beyond Peoria Avenue, 11th bends southwest and becomes 10th Street. Follow the S-curve into 12th Street. Then, at the stop, turn south and follow Southwest Boulevard across the bridge. You may take Southwest Boulevard into **Sapulpa,** if you wish. A quicker and easier route is to rejoin the Free Road just before Southwest becomes Sapulpa Road and bends west. The overpass to 60th Street will take you across to the east side of I-44. Follow signs for the Free Road (SR 66 and 33) toward Sapulpa where the older alignment returns. There's no advantage to the turnpike here since SR 66 is very well maintained.

Like Tulsa, Sapulpa has learned to use art cosmetically. Empty store windows become display points for photographic prints. Boarded-up windows in the side of a two-story building become a hand-painted triptych. If you're getting hungry, Norma's Cafe—run by the real Norma—has been serving roadies for years.

Departing Sapulpa, watch for an old steel-truss bridge off to the right, about a mile west of town. It's just beyond an intersection marked, curiously enough, Highway 66 and Old Highway 66—perhaps the only acknowledgment of both alignments anywhere in the country. The bridge is especially photogenic with its well-preserved, red-brick deck. Continue on the older alignment beyond the bridge, if you like. It's easy to rejoin SR 66 a few miles farther on, at SR 33.

From Sapulpa through **Kellyville, Bristow,** and **Depew,** there are a number of abandoned sections of old, old Route 66 on the northwest side of the Free Road, some of which can be driven for short distances.

There are also a couple of very nice loops of older alignment, beginning about two miles beyond Kellyville. The first is just past the interstate overpass and rates a slow, top-down drive. There's also another angular section a few miles farther on. It's said that there was once an old airfield along the west leg of this loop. No one has spotted it yet, though. Maybe, you'll be the first. So do some exploring and find your own favorite little tree-shaded country lane. Remember to keep an eye out for lines of weathered telephone poles and old cuts through the trees.

Rolling on into **Stroud,** be sure to check the Rock Cafe to see if it has reopened. It was for years a twenty-four-hour must-stop for travelers through this area. Down the street, 66 Antiques is worth a browse. If the name Stroud sounds a little tough for this sleepy little town now, it's because the place once really was tough. Cattle drovers shipped from here, the nearby Indian Territory was dry, and a string of bars made lots of money selling hooch of questionable character to everybody. Now Stroud is the kind of place where, if you are doing a late wash, you lock up the laundromat after yourself. Nice town.

Approaching **Davenport,** continue straight at the curve for the center of town. Locals take some pride in their rolling streets here. Main is known as Snuff Street —"drive a block and take a dip." Beyond Davenport, the old route heads on into **Chandler.**

Entering Chandler on First Street, the Lincoln Motel on the right has been meticulously maintained since it was built in 1939. If there's a vacancy, it'll hit all your history-buttons. Preservation and restoration is well supported in Chandler. There's even talk of doing something special with the old armory. Angling south on Manvel, notice the well-kept vintage gas station and some of the restoration already completed downtown. Midway through town, on the right, is a fine old bakery for your coffee break or Granny's restaurant for a meal. Both are excellent. Leaving town, the road bends west again—past an abandoned truck on the left, which looks as though it has a terrible headache—and heads toward Luther.

If you're driving something like a Mustang GT or a Corvette, there are some perfectly banked left and right sweepers through this section that can make you cry for more good old roads. Clearly, this highway was designed by men who drove, not by men who budgeted. And it's not hard to tell the difference in the result, is it?

At **Arcadia,** make a slow circle through this little town. It still has that 1920s feeling and in an old motel,

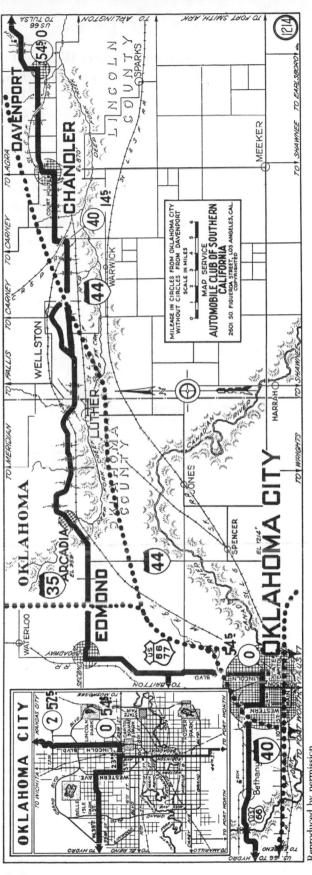

Bob's BBQ is now a foodie's landmark. The Round
Barn, which has stood on the bluff here since before the
turn of the century, needs additional restoration but
fund-raising is hard for a tiny town like this, and it's
slow going.

From Arcadia, continue west, but take care. This
section of road has not been well maintained in the
past. Cross I-35 and head on into **Edmond,** now a
northern suburb of Oklahoma City. Little of the old
Route 66 feeling remains here. But Edmond is a college
town, enjoys a lovely campus, and is a pleasant place in
which to shop or take care of business before the run
down to **Oklahoma City.** If you plan to bypass
Oklahoma City, however, it's easier to take I-35 in,
junction with I-44, and continue west to the Bethany
exit.

Oklahoma City
to Texola

From Second Street in Edmond, turn south on
Broadway (US 77) and continue toward the city, jogging
east at the Kelley Avenue exit, and turn south again to
enter Oklahoma City on Kelley. At 63rd Street,
however, you may wish to satisfy your baser instincts by
turning east to the National Cowboy Hall of Fame, just
west of I-35, and/or the Oklahoma County Line
Restaurant, a half mile farther west, both on the north
side of I-44.

The Hall of Fame may even be a case of western
overawe. But the County Line is hog-heaven for
barbecue fans. Once known as the secretive Kentucky
Club, a racy gambling den and roadhouse for the likes
of Pretty Boy Floyd, the County Line sports hidden
trapdoors in each of the tiny side rooms that surround
the main eatery and bar. Ernest Hemingway would have
loved this place. The beef ribs? Aficionados call them
dinosaur ribs. And the doggie bags here look like clothes
hampers. Check in early, though. The County Line is a
secret no longer.

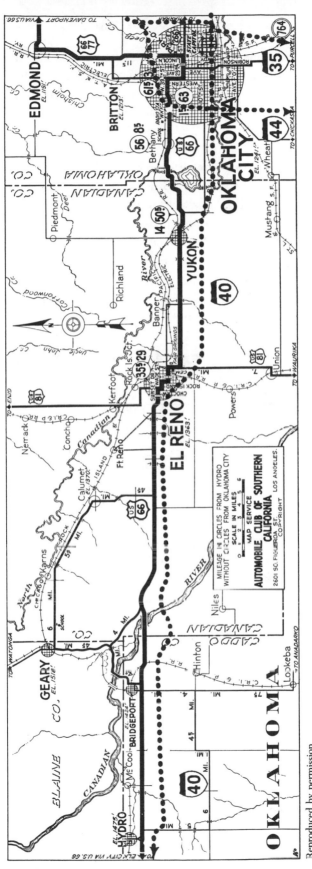

Reproduced by permission

Heading on into the city, jog west on 50th Street to Lincoln Boulevard (US 77) southbound. Skirt the capitol, staying to the right, and take 23rd Street. Continue on Route 66 by following 23rd to Classen. Turn north, go past the giant milk bottle, and roll on up to westbound I-44 for an easy way out of town.

Route 66 is always evolving. Old businesses, often sadly, close. So a newer road-related business is cause for some celebration. And one of the brightest of the newer enterprises is just ahead. At the top of Classen, turn west on Northwest Highway (SR 3A) a half mile. Here, on the third floor of 50 Penn Place, just across from Penn Square Mall, you'll find Route 66 (the shop) and a treasure trove of collectibles, handmade jewelry, original photographs, and US 66 memorabilia—plus everything from a neon chair to a couch fashioned from the rear deck of a classic '50s automobile. "Wildly eclectic—boldly elegant" say the two young women and their artist partner of their collection. And it is, indeed, eclectic. But it is the ladies themselves who are elegant. And witty, and warm, and of a kindly disposition toward travelers in from the road. If you're looking for that special, take-home item from your tour of the old highway, Route 66 is a wonderful place to search through. And if you need a moment to decide, drop in at the Full Circle bookstore just across the way. It's a charming browsery and an ideal companion to the Route 66 shop. Then, when you're ready, head west on I-44.

To rejoin the old route, exit at 39th Street (SR 66), if you're in the mood for a little lakeside cruise and a picnic. Pick up some victuals in **Bethany** and head west again on 39th Street. After crossing Council Road, jog south to take the old North Canadian River bridge. There are a couple of nice spots on Lake Overholser's north shore.

Back in 1941, this lake was the first and only body of water in Oklahoma to be officially designated as a seaplane base. Pan American Airways' graceful Clippers were all the rage then and transcontinental seaplane travel was considered to be the next major development in air travel. But by the time World War II had ended, military and civilian engineers had built thousands of miles of long concrete runways almost everywhere. The seaplane era was over, even for small craft, and Lake Overholser's hopes faded with the times.

At the far side of the lake, bear right at the **Y**-intersection and head west to Mustang Road. Jog north and take the four-lane westbound to **Yukon.**

If you happen to be in Yukon near day's end, do wait until dusk when the huge, newly restored chase lights come on atop the big Yukon Flour Mill. Watch the sign for a while. It has more than charm; it can mesmerize you.

If you need to continue on the interstate through this section, you may still connect with at least a little of the history of old Route 66 by stopping at Hensley's, just off I-40 at the Country Club Road exit. A family gas-and-food operation on Route 66, dating from 1939, Hensley's moved to its present location after thirty years on the old road as Consumers Cafe. The food is still good and if you stay over, breakfast is on the house. Another Hensley tradition.

Approaching **El Reno** on the old highway, watch for the Big 8 Motel, advertising itself as AMARILLO'S FINEST. And no, the owners are not confused. The sign is a legacy from the movie *Rain Man,* part of which was shot here. In fact you can stay in the room—set-dressed just as it was—featured in the film. Just ask for Room 117. You'll even be checked in by the same fellow (only a little typecasting here) who played the desk clerk in the picture. Now all you need is a 1949 Buick with portholes. Or Dustin's phone number.

Dynaflowing on west, continue straight, or for the older alignment turn north on Sheppard at the signal, then curve west along the cemetery on Elm. At the water tower signal, turn north on Rock Island (US 81N). Just a few blocks along, on the right side, is the remarkable BPOE Lodge. This building was once part of an Oklahoma territorial exhibit (remember, Oklahoma was not yet a state) at the St. Louis Exposition of 1904 —the fair that introduced the world to hot dogs and ice cream. Next to chili, that's about as American as you can get. When the exhibit closed, the building was disassembled and brought to El Reno as a permanent structure. If the Elks are not the Best People On Earth, as their sign suggests, they are certainly among the most industrious.

At Wade, turn west again, then north on Choctaw and west on Sunset. Continue west, then bear right just after the sign for **Fort Reno,** and short of the entrance to westbound I-40. Another quick right will take you up to Fort Reno itself. But unless a special event is planned, there is little cause to linger.

Heading west, there are two choices, as you'll see from the accompanying map. You may continue due west on the 1932 alignment or turn north for **Calumet** and **Geary.** Unless you have plenty of time, the straight-arrow route is better. Beyond the US 270 junction, continue west, bearing northwest at the Y-intersection. Follow Spur 281 to the next Y and bear southwest. Then be ready for a treat as you approach a bridge of no fewer than thirty-eight—count 'em, thirty-eight—spans.

There are lots of roadie explanations for the number of spans here: frequent washouts, the weight of tank convoys, a steel shortage, and so on. But the truth is that each of these spans is simply as large as the highway department's early equipment could lift into place. Of course, you can stick with the tank convoy story if it works better for you. Part of traveling is taking home whatever stories you like.

From **Bridgeport,** continue west toward **Hydro.** Take care, however, for the road has several dipsy-doodles through this section, punctuated by short, unexpected stretches of gravel. There are a couple of old, live-over gas stations along here as well, one closed, one still operating. But it's the road itself that is really the main attraction here. Pink, tree-shaded concrete with the innocent-looking little half curbs that were once so innovative. The trouble was that the curbs accomplished more than was intended by highway engineers.

Instead of promoting drainage, they could turn a hill face into a solid sheet of water during a hard rain —which is the only kind of rain Oklahoma seems to have. If you got between two such hills, you'd likely stay there until the weather cleared. Sometimes other folks would come slithering down to the bottom, too, making an even bigger mess.

The other thing the curbs were intended to do was to redirect errant autos back onto the roadway. The curbs managed that, too. But many cars were tossed over onto their tops in the process. Not surprising you don't see a lot of this kind of curbing anymore.

Approaching **Weatherford** on the north service road of I-40, make a quick jog south onto westbound Main Street via Washington Avenue. To the north a few blocks is Southwestern Oklahoma State University. Overlooking the town, the site is all the more attractive for its early architecture, recalling the days when it served only as a teachers' college. The campus remains one of the prettiest anywhere along the route.

Unless they are, the Out to Lunch Cafe on the right at midtown is a good spot if you're ready to have a light meal and regroup. Nice folks, good food, and pretty, down-home waitresses who aren't required to babble their names as part of a spiel to push the daily special. Here, they'll just smile that wonderful Oklahoma *Hi-y'all* smile and let you make up your own mind. Next best thing to sharing the front-porch swing and a lemonade with your sweetie.

Departing Weatherford, continue straight west as the state highway curves southwest, and turn south on 4th Street (SR 54). Follow the sharp bend west and continue on old Route 66 on the north side of I-40. Cross over at the T-intersection, turn west at the stop, and continue on the south side beyond the next interchange.

Return to the north side as necessary and continue on the four-lane into **Clinton,** entering on Choctaw Avenue. Pop Hicks Restaurant, on the right a few blocks farther, is the local chat-and-chew and has been a Route 66 landmark since 1936. It's like a town bulletin board with silverware. For the city route, turn south on 4th Street, then west on Frisco Avenue. Main Street America doesn't get much nicer than Clinton, so take time to enjoy.

Most Elvis sightings on old Route 66 have a

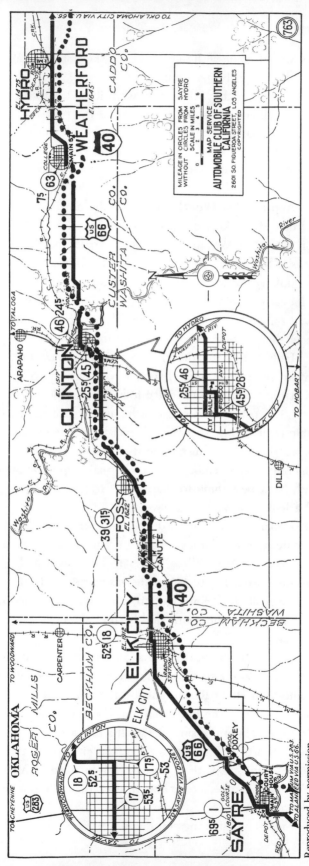

Reproduced by permission

distinct UFO quality, but you really can sleep in a room where Elvis stayed, at the Trade Winds Courtyard Inn. Or, if Elvis isn't your style, they might have a Margaret O'Brien Room. You could ask.

Leaving Clinton, there is a definite scenery-or-food choice to make. To follow old Route 66, turn south on 10th Street and continue as it becomes Neptune Drive. Bear west at the **Y**, to the right of the old motel and roadhouse, and head west on Commerce Road.

But if your lip is set for a world-class barbecue sandwich on a bun the size of Delaware, make tracks for the interstate and Jiggs Smokehouse. Jiggs used to advertise on a billboard along the highway, but most of the sign fell down some years ago. Didn't matter, though. The place is so well known now that customers from both coasts show up regularly for their barbecue-beef fix. Even grab-it-and-go people, who don't usually notice their food or care that much for barbecue, end up way down the highway, licking the waxed paper and regretting the miles. Jiggs is on the north side of I-40 at the Parkersburg Road exit just west of Clinton. Come and set a spell.

West Commerce Road leads to the Stafford Exit, where you may continue on the north service road, recrossing to the south side at Clinton Lake Road and crossing again to the north side just beyond the railroad, or head for **Elk City** on I-40. Enter Elk City on the four-lane, continuing west a mile and a half to the exit just beyond the T-33 jet. Jog west on Country Club, continuing to the park, then turn south at the church onto Main Street. Follow Main to Broadway, turn west, and continue to the **T** at Pioneer. Jog one block north, then turn west on Third. At the intersection is a museum and a pleasant park with a train ride for kids.

If it's lunchtime, however, you'll want to head back down Third to the Country Dove, a gift shop and tearoom extraordinaire. Oklahoma is not, as you may have discovered, a souper's paradise. But even if a light vegetarian lunch rings no bells for you, the French Silk pie will. This dessert is so light, it's like sampling chocolate air and will leave you wondering whether you should use a fork or just smear it right on your body.

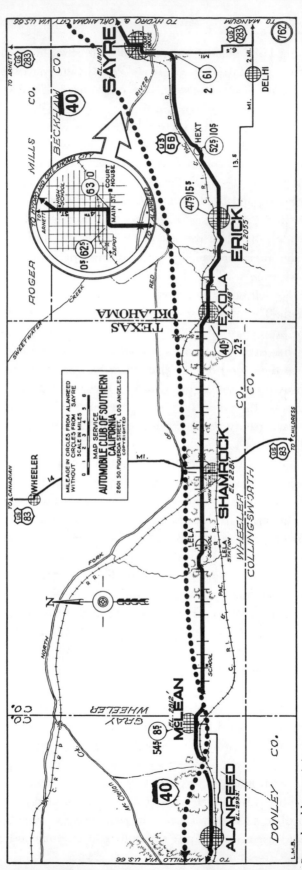

To continue on the older alignment, jog right onto the north frontage road just before the I-40 entrance, crossing to the south side after four and a half miles, and recrossing to the north side at Cemetery Road. Continue on into **Sayre,** turning right at the stop onto Business Loop 40. Through Sayre, bear south on Fourth Street (US 283) and follow it directly across Red River (whence the movie of the same name) without jogging west on Main, where the older bridge is closed.

It was at the old Route 66 bridge in Sayre that the Great Indian Uprising of 1959 is said to have occurred. The bridge itself had burned and was barricaded. But as each out-of-state car slowed for the detour, Sayre high school students excitedly told the tourists to roll up their windows and head west as fast as possible because Indians had burned the bridge and were on the warpath. For the better part of a day, the Oklahoma Highway Patrol had its hands full stopping all the speeding cars headed for Texas—and safety from all those rampaging Indians.

Heading west at a more leisurely pace, turn onto the north frontage road a mile beyond the present bridge, crossing under I-40 to the south side and continuing west into **Erick.** This pleasant, helpful town also had a speeding problem, but it was no joke. In fact, Erick had become known as one of the worst speed traps in the nation. Using a speedy black 1938 Ford with Oklahoma overdrive, Officer Elmer could catch just about anyone he had a mind to. When he once busted Bob Hope, the comedian quipped on his next radio show that the only way he'd go through Erick again would be on a donkey.

But Officer Elmer's prowess soon proved too much for the town. Tourist business had fallen off badly, and Elmer had to go—at least officially. But on dark nights, some travelers along this stretch of road say that an old black Ford V-8 still has a way of appearing suddenly in the rearview mirror. Just a warning, perhaps.

Further down the road in **Texola,** it was a different tale. A few years before, there had been travelers and truck drivers all over the place. Never a boisterous town, folks there awakened one morning to find that some pranksters had climbed up to a huge TEXOLA sign facing onto the highway. There, they'd simply changed the T to an S. Within hours, strangers were making purchases just to ask where the house (as in *house*) was located.

There is only a foundation now where the welcoming sign with the saucy message once stood. But if you scrunch up your eyes a little, it's not hard to imagine how inviting that sign must have looked to someone long on the road and far from home.

CHAPTER
5

Texas

Without a river or some continental rift, border crossings between states usually pass without notice. But not here. Almost immediately after entering Texas, the land changes. It's almost as if someone looked carefully at this place and decided, without regard for political interests, that the state line just naturally belonged right *here*.

Leaving the rolling, wooded hills of Oklahoma, the Panhandle of Texas opens like an immense natural stage. In the space of a few miles the land becomes flatter, more angular, a little threatening. Not a good place to have a horse pull up lame if you were a line-rider. Not a good place to have your clapped-out old truck throw a rod if you were an Okie family trying gamely with your little ones to reach California. Not a gentle place at all. But a place magnificent, like the sea, in its sheer, endless expanse. And in the way the land challenges you to open yourself to it, to take it all in—or scuttle quickly across to an easier region.

Few places in America scrape at primitive human emotions the way Texas does. People who live on this land are afflicted either with the fierce loyalty known only to those who have learned to hold adversity lightly in their hands, or the equally burning desire to get the hell out of here.

Even the remnant of old Route 66 has a hunkered-down look as it climbs toward the breaks just west of Alanreed. Beyond these crumbling bluffs the high plains begin in earnest. A few miles more and the tumbled character of the land disappears almost completely, surrendering to a vast, treeless plain that flattens the entire horizon all the way into New Mexico.

Windy, dry, appearing virtually limitless, even to the 65-mile-an-hour eye, the distances seem endless:

> The sun has riz,
> The sun has set,
> And here we is
> In Texas yet.

So convinced were the earliest travelers that they were in imminent danger of simply becoming lost to death out here that they drove stakes into even the slightest rise to point the way. Coming upon these frail markers, riders from the south named this region Llano Estacado—the Staked Plain.

As you cross this land now with relative ease, imagine yourself out here alone, in an earlier time. Stakes or no, could you have walked this two-hundred-mile stretch in search of something better than you had back home? Would you have done that? Interesting to notice what a tight grasp old Demon Comfort can have on us, isn't it?

But rather than just looking through the windshield at what lies everywhere around, take a few minutes out in the open along this stretch of road, or down by Claude, or out near Adrian, beyond Amarillo. Walk for a bit, away from your car-cocoon and the certainty of a smooth, predictable highway. Even a few yards will do—toward whatever spot announces itself to you.

Get acquainted with the wind. No words, no other

medium, can convey what earlier passers-through must have felt here on this land. But the wind still communicates it perfectly. So find that spot, walk out to it, and clear your mind for a few minutes. Notice what you're feeling as you stand facing into a wind older than the plain itself. Take just a moment to know something of this land before you move on. Sense what it means to be out here.

In Texas.

Shamrock to Adrian

Continue on the south service road from Texola, entering **Shamrock** on Business Loop 40. At the junction with US 83, be sure U Drop Inn, as the name once suggested, and you'll find a friendly spot for a coffee break. You'll also find this service station complex, dating from 1936, is one of the finest examples of art deco architecture on all of old Route 66. Shamrock, once a booming oil and gas center, celebrates its Irish heritage. But somehow the image is muddled. A leprechaun in chaps? Duke Wayne in a green derby hat?

Continuing west, it's easier to take the interstate. You'll see portions of old Route 66, particularly on the south side of I-40, but most sections are isolated or difficult to reach. **McLean** is one of the nicer towns in the Panhandle, however, so you may want to exit. Life is slower paced here. On Sunday morning, people on the way to church all take care to wave hello to a stranger. Small towns like this were once the extended families of America. McLean still is.

During World War II, there was a German POW camp just east of town. On weekends, some of the prisoners were released for a movie and perhaps a chocolate soda at the Rexall drugstore. A few people have always been upset by that, not truly recognizing that POWs are not felons, nor that the prisoners

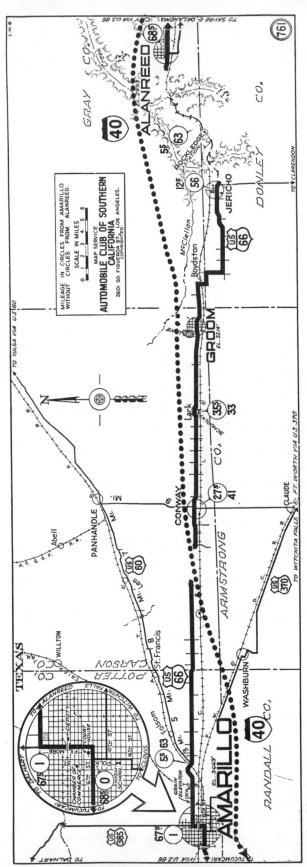

Reproduced by permission

wouldn't try to leave anyway. For even if they somehow
made it back to Germany, they'd only have been sent to
serve on the Russian front—a virtual death sentence in
itself. Still, a POW camp with such a release policy
usually earned the name "Fritz Ritz."

Departing McLean, follow old Route 66 on the
south side of I-40 through **Alanreed,** then return to
I-40. Further west, near **Groom,** the Britten USA
water tower is sure to get your attention. And that's
just what it was intended to do. How many folks do
you suppose buy a little of this and that when they stop
to ask about this leaning tower of Texas? Not exactly
classy, but it is marketing in the best roadside tradition.

If you're getting a little tired of the interstate, you
may want to take the next exit south to **Claude,**
through which the original 1926–27 alignment of Route
66 passed, returning to I-40 via US 287. Then continue
on to Exit 75, in **Amarillo,** if you want to try your
luck at hustling one of the humongous 72-ounce steaks
at the Big Texan Steak Ranch. The smart money says
you can't do it, but what the hell? It's one of the safer
games in town.

For more advanced cases of the kind of too-flat
fever this section of highway can sometimes induce,
head south on I-27 and turn east at **Canyon** on SR
217. Here, less than half an hour from Amarillo, is one
of the most beautiful areas to be found anywhere in the
Southwest: Palo Duro Canyon.

It's as if Nature felt that the Panhandle plains
needed some bit of contrast—an exception to prove
the rule. If so, Palo Duro is certainly that. The colors,
in haunting desert tints, and the unexpected formations
of this canyon are unique. Hiking trails are well laid
out, along with miles of scenic drives and bridle paths.
Horses are available and there is even a miniature
narrow-gauge railroad for the youngsters. The canyon
area is at its best just before twilight and in the early
morning, so plan on an overnight in Amarillo, if
possible.

To follow the old city route through Amarillo,
take Business Loop 40 on Amarillo Boulevard (Exit 85).
There is a strong feeling of old Route 66 along this
stretch, though it becomes a little ticky-tacky closer to

town. But don't sell Amarillo short. It's one of the most underrated cities along old Route 66 and worth some time. Since part of the original route is now one-way, turn south on Pierce Street and then west again on 6th Street. There are a number of interesting Route 66–era businesses along this section and the local merchants' association is now working hard to recapture something of the old highway's flavor through town. Most recently, a revitalization study of the West 6th Street area was completed to attract more local support.

Originally, this area was part of the suburb of **San Jacinto Heights** and it still bears some of the feeling of Texas towns where the Bible Belt runs head on into the Wild West tradition. Rooming houses employing, according to one Amarillo city official, "ladies of whenever" were sometimes exorcised when the property changed hands in order to drive off whatever naughty spirits might remain. Yet while they operated, these houses sat cheek-by-hog-jowl with a family restaurant where the original Pig Hip sandwich was created in 1930.

Not too far away, the Amarillo Natatorium offered indoor swimming as at least a temporary respite from summertime heat. Truly a Panhandle phenomenon, The Nat looked like an architectural Appaloosa horse—with a graystone Moorish-Camelot front half joined to a porthole-dotted steamship posterior. Although the pool concept didn't pan out, The Nat did become an outstanding attraction as a ballroom. Reopening in 1926 (the same year in which Route 66 was chartered), The Nat hosted the top bands of the '30s and '40s—Paul Whiteman, Count Basie, Louis Armstrong, Benny Goodman, and Harry James. Not bad for a former swimming hole.

But West 6th Street is probably best remembered for its Texas-style, shoot-from-the-hip marketing. During hard times, one grocer took to announcing his daily specials to shoppers from the rooftop of his building. And the way he got the crowd's attention was by tossing live chickens off the roof. Now, while it's a fact that chickens in their natural state can do a little flying, these were market-ready, clipped-wing models with all the flight characteristics of a feathered rock.

From the roof, about the best anyone could expect was a barely controlled free-fall. So, if you were headed for this grocery, you had to be prepared. And you probably had to like chicken a lot.

The Chicken Follies are gone now—and just as well—but you'll find much of interest before leaving this part of Amarillo. Jogging southwest on Bushland and then west on 9th Avenue, continue on out of town. West of Amarillo, old Route 66 exists only as the north service road for I-40, just a few yards away, so there is little advantage in taking the old road, which rejoins the interstate beyond **Vega** and **Adrian.**

As you drive west from Amarillo, however, do keep watch for a row of ten Cadillacs—in various stages of fin—augered methodically into the land just south of the interstate. Although it looks as if it could have been left by Druids, Cadillac Ranch was in fact placed here by pop-art financier Stanley Marsh, 3. It may also be the clearest visual statement ever about wretched excess in oil-propelled America. Try as we will to ignore the message of these iron dinosaurs, we cannot.

Change your ways, they say in mute eloquence, *or join us.*

CHAPTER
6

New Mexico

New Mexico is descended from the sky. Other places along old Route 66 have been formed from rivers, mountains, and plains. Other states have been forged by iron-willed men meeting in urgency behind closed doors to make a truce, a compromise, a set of defensible boundaries. But New Mexico has no door on its history, no roof on its being. The first allegiance of most people here is to the land and to the generous sky above. Boundaries here seem best determined where these two—earth and sky—meet.

In the New Mexican view, cities are to be used as gathering points—for art as much as commerce—and not for population centers or power bases. Santa Fe is older than any city of Colonial America, and has been a capital for more than three hundred years, yet its population barely tops 75,000. The oldest public building in the United States is here in Santa Fe. Yet even with such a head start, the city refuses to have a proper airport. Newcomers rarely understand this until they have lived here for a while. Then they realize why there is no major airline operation in Santa Fe . . . It would interfere with the sky.

In New Mexico, travelers along old Route 66 begin to notice something different in the sky above about the time they reach Tucumcari. The color—a deeper, more translucent lens of cobalt blue—can take even experienced color photographers by surprise. No wonder the painters, and after them the writers, began migrating here well before Route 66 first made its way across the state. Driving through New Mexico's high country in crackling bright sunshine, or rolling through one of the long valleys with billowing rain clouds so close overhead they seem almost touchable, everything here seems to put you at stage center. You always seem to be right in the middle of the performance.

It's easy for a traveler to get religion—any kind— in a place like New Mexico, where earth and sky and wind and water greet one another in such unexpected ways. All the simple distinctions of mind, former notions about what is and what isn't, begin to blur. Following old Route 66 at a slower pace through the eastern hills, across the Continental Divide and into serious mesa country, perceptions change. It's easier here, as an observer, to become part of all that is being observed, to feel a sense of connection with everything around. As a traveler, it is easier to slip loose from the sense of detachment and not-belonging that often seems to be a part of any great crossing.

This enchanted land asks little of you as a traveler, except one thing. It asks that you allow yourself to become enchanted, too.

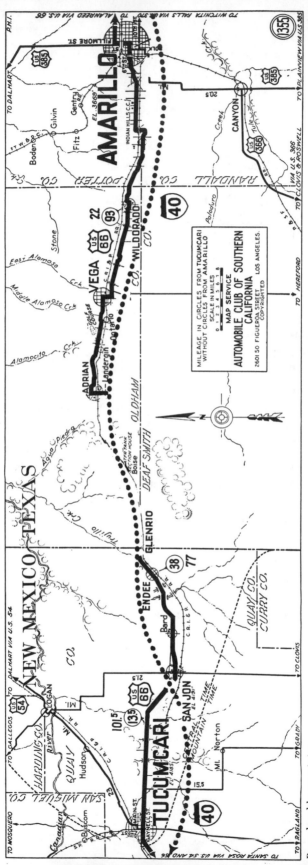

Glenrio to Albuquerque

Although the sign for a business loop through **Glenrio** may be somewhat misleading, this nearly empty town remains one of the most charming vestiges along old Route 66. The well-known Last Motel in Texas/First Motel in Texas flourished just east of the state line. But its sign has faded and fallen, along with the hopes and dreams of another bypassed town. The old route does continue on into **San Jon,** but if you wish to visit there, it's best to avoid the old road, which has been covered over with slippery gravel, and rejoin the interstate for a few miles. Then, at San Jon, return to the old road on the south side and continue west toward **Tucumcari,** crossing to the north side just before town.

For most old Route 66 travelers, the *real* West began with some simple but meaningful event. For some it was the first glimpse of the long, low, fencelike sign for Whiting Brothers. For others, it was arriving in Tucumcari. City of 2,000 rooms. The only place to spend tonight. With powerful roadside advertising it was tough to pass Tucumcari by, and few did. Following Business Loop 40 (Gaynell Street on the accompanying map), you'll see many survivors: The Tee Pee, Blue Swallow, Palomino. Sweet reminders, still among us.

Heading west, continue on the south-side service road. After several miles, you must return to I-40 until the stretch from **Montoya** through **Newkirk** to **Cucrvo**—three dear but near-death towns, strung out along old Route 66 like amulets on an antique Spanish chain.

This is part of a very old route, the first New Mexico road begun with federal aid, back in 1918. The tiny grocery stores were not only tourist stops but the center of life here, connecting travelers, townspeople, and those who have always roamed these barrancas. Richardson's Store & Good Gulf, Knowles Grocery, Wilkerson's, all way stations for regular long-haul rigs,

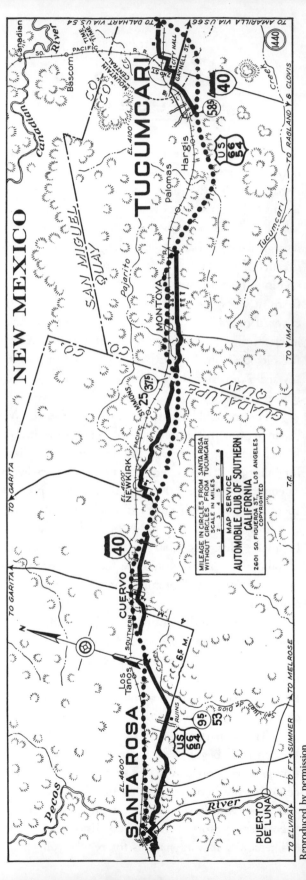

Reproduced by permission

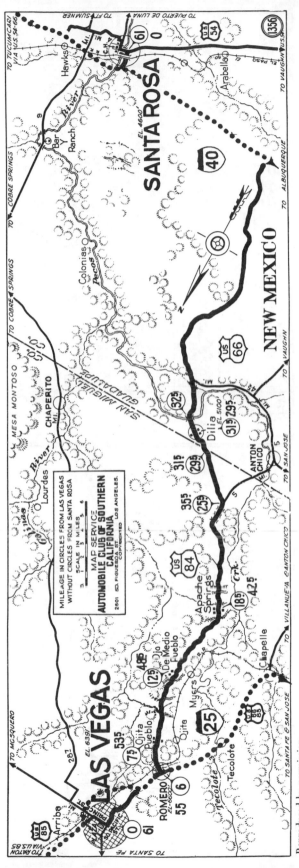

Reproduced by permission

touring cars, ponies, and daily school buses. Hanging on, hoping for a Route 66 revival. But like the hand-painted signs on the old clapboard siding, fading fast.

From Cuervo, the old alignment has been in terrible condition for some time. So unless repairs have been made, it's better to take the interstate west to the first exit for **Santa Rosa.** Follow the old road into town on Will Rogers Drive. Santa Rosa is also a Route 66 landmark in itself. But unlike Tucumcari, Santa Rosa needed far less advertising. Santa Rosa has the weather.

Probably more people have been snowbound in Santa Rosa than in any other place on old Route 66 west of St. Louis. The old road, with its tail-twisting route, was far more difficult than the newer highway to keep clear. And with snow removal equipment at a premium in this desert state, folks caught in blizzard conditions around here tended to stay put.

That's usually when they discovered that Santa Rosa wasn't such a bad spot in which to be stranded. Especially if they were within snow-trudging distance of the Club Cafe, a haven for Route 66 travelers since 1935. The Cafe has greeted strangers via Fat Man billboards, postcards, and the airwaves of KSYX (get it?) for years. So, if you should see a skywriter doing welcome signs in the blue above, you'll know who's behind it.

Heading out of town, there are two major choices of route: directly west to Albuquerque, largely via I-40 to Moriarty, or the pre-1937 alignment through **Santa Fe.** Both routes are interesting and colorful. The loop north is partly over I-25 and takes about a half day longer.

If Santa Fe is your preference, turn north on US 84 west of Santa Rosa, which joins the old Route 66 alignment near **Dilia,** and continue to the junction with I-25 at Romero, now **Romeroville.** To rejoin the old route at **Pecos,** take the interstate westbound to the SR 63 exit. Continue north to Pecos and give yourself a moment to unwind here in the tall country. Though the town is quiet now, there was a major real estate boom just two miles southwest of here, in about A.D. 1100, when the Pecos Pueblo stood five stories high.

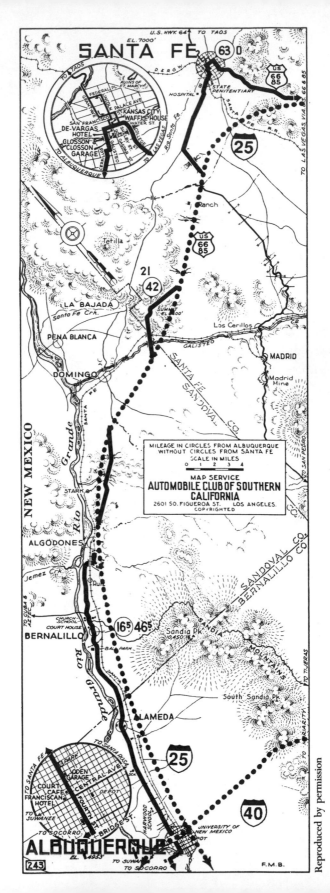

Continuing southwest on SR 50, you must rejoin I-25 briefly.

At the Apache Canyon/Cañoncito Exit, follow the old route into Santa Fe. Enter the city on Old Santa Fe/ Pecos Trail (formerly College Street), crossing the river to the Plaza. Santa Fe is one of the most unique of all American cities, so take some time to stroll the Plaza. There are so many fine restaurants and galleries here, you could easily eat and art yourself into oblivion in just a couple of days. Try La Fonda for breakfast, The Shed or La Tertulia for lunch and, just a few miles north, El Nido or El Rancho Encantado for supper. For an overnight stay, El Rey Inn offers both pleasant and inexpensive ambiance from the '30s and '40s. Or, for a memorable night of special charm, reserve a room at the timeless Inn on the Alameda—one of the most quietly elegant and romantic places to be found anywhere.

Departing Santa Fe from the Plaza, just follow the Don Gaspar Avenue, De Vargas Street, Galisteo Street, and Cerillos Road alignment as shown on the accompanying map. It's a good route and Santa Fe doesn't tinker with what works. Follow Cerillos onto I-25 and continue south.

Just off the route, about halfway to **Algodones,** is a tiny bit of another world and as remarkable a place as you're likely to find. It's the Santo Domingo Indian Trading Post, a couple of miles west of the interstate. Half hidden in a stand of cottonwood trees, wedged in between Galisteo Creek and the railroad tracks near **Domingo,** Fred Thompson's place is one of a kind. *Life* magazine once came here to do a piece. And his curiosity aroused, President Kennedy turned up here in 1962. You can buy nearly anything but the old Frazer sedan that has been sitting out front for thirty years. How about a few postcards and a soda? Some Dr. McLean's Volcanic Liniment? You also might check the names in the 5,000-page guest register—it's even money that some neighbor of yours once visited here, too.

Continuing south on I-25, take the Algodones Exit for the old route (SR 313) through **Bernalillo** and **Alameda.** Nearing **Albuquerque,** the road becomes

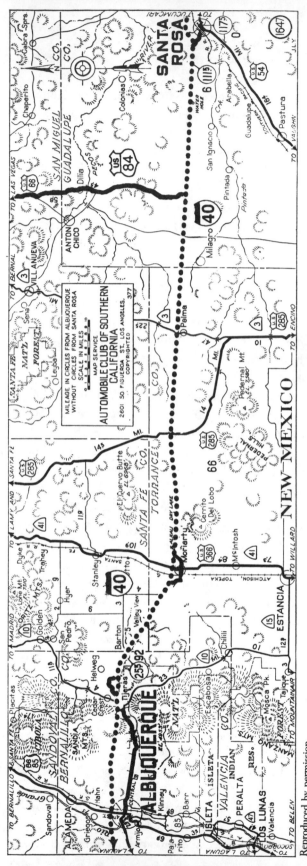

SR 556 and 4th Street. Follow 4th to Bridge Boulevard, jog west for the Barelas Bridge, and south again on Isleta Boulevard (SR 314). Turn west on SR 6 in **Los Lunas** and continue to the junction with I-40 at Correo. This route, with everything from near-zero traffic density to a row of baby volcanoes, also offers an occasional glimpse of old, old, old Route 66 to the south.

If you've chosen the more direct route to Correo (formerly Suwanee) via **Clines Corners, Moriarty, Tijeras,** and Albuquerque, continue west from Santa Rosa on I-40. On the way, take a moment for the old Longhorn Ranch at Exit 203. Although the cluster of buildings here was not typical of the early mom-and-pop kind of roadside attraction that flourished along old Route 66, the Longhorn does sport some of the carnival feeling that nearly every tourist attraction had. Returning to the interstate, continue to the Moriarty exit and follow the old route through town. From Tijeras follow one or another of the old alignments into Albuquerque.

Both the old highway and the newer interstate look easily laid out through this area, but that is part of the road builder's art. Because Tijeras Canyon was such tough going, new construction has often been delayed on this section. Consider a report from the New Mexico Highway Department from as late as 1951. It described the result of setting off dynamite charges in a thousand holes that had been laboriously drilled in one small area. That's a *thousand* charges set off simultaneously. A big bang, all right. But here's the clincher. After all that, there was so little debris that it took only twenty minutes to clear it all up.

If you've stayed on the interstate, you can exit for the business loop at Central Avenue. However, there is very little feeling of old Route 66 along the eastern reaches of Central Avenue. A route that leaves more time for touring the downtown section is to exit at San Mateo Avenue (SR 367) southbound and turn west again on Central. Local revitalization projects have done wonders in preserving and maintaining charming shops and businesses in the downtown area. Lindy's has been serving up an agreeable chili since 1929. And the 66

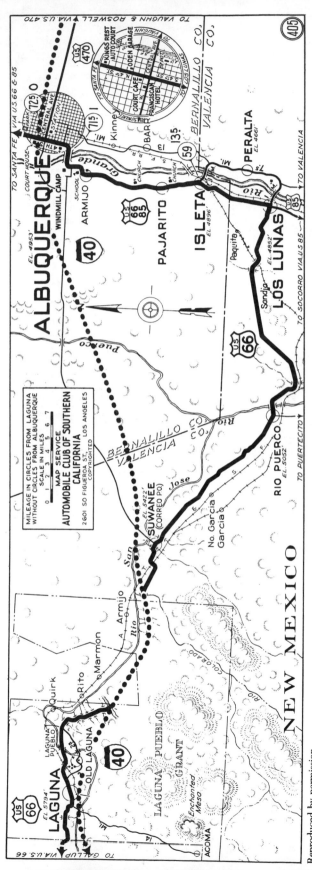

Diner crew has put together a great nouveau-'50s eatery, where the chocolate malteds are almost better than memory. Even the meat loaf comes from the recipe of a woman who loved to cook and knew how to do so.

Motel properties have fared less well but there are still survivors like El Vado, with its magnificent neon. One of the earliest and best of Albuquerque's restorations is the lovely KiMo Theater. Originally built by the Boller Brothers, a theater design group with a reputation in the Southwest for a kind of Hi-Ho Rococo style, this theater is truly a window into the golden era of both roads and theaters in America. Fully restored, it stands as a bellwether enterprise and a model of what can and should be accomplished elsewhere along old Route 66.

Albuquerque to Manuelito

After crossing the Old Town Bridge westbound, continue up Nine-Mile Hill, so called because its crest is exactly that distance from Albuquerque's center. If it's early morning or evening, or if there are clouds over the Sandia Mountains to the east, it's worth a photo stop near the top of the hill.

You can follow the old route as it flanks I-40 west to **Correo,** but the only difference is a fence between the two. At the Rio Puerco crossing, however, it's worth an exit just to inspect and photograph the old bridge, though the nearby trading post may be closed. It's hard to understand how this tiny section of the old route manages to seem such an island in time with the interstate so close by. But it does.

Continuing west on the interstate, take the **Laguna** (SR 124) exit for a superb section of old Route 66. This stretch of road is a little slower than SR 6 from Los Lunas, but has more feeling of the Southwest during the 1930s and '40s than nearly any other part of

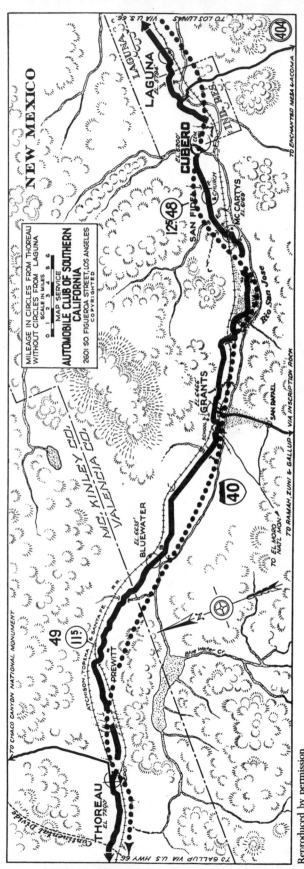

the old route. There's also much to be rediscovered
here, so take your time. At the Laguna Pueblo, jog
south to follow the older alignment until it returns to
the four-lane. This little loop, especially, is like driving
right into an old View-Master scene.

Approaching **Budville,** bear north with the old
alignment, which passes through **Cubero** and returns.
It was at nearby Villa Cubero that Ernest Hemingway
settled in with his notebooks to write a major part of
The Old Man and the Sea. He knew as well as anyone that
the quality of human perception depends on contrast. If
you are going to write about something like the sea,
one way to hold the vision of that sea in stark relief is
to go as far from it as you can. Cubero filled the bill.

Crossing to the south side of I-40 from Cubero,
the old route continues past **McCartys.** A little farther
on it recrosses to the north side, SR 124 ends, and
you'll rejoin I-40 to the **Grants** exit. If you're among
the many who are traveling in summer, you may want
to head south from Grants to the perpetual Ice Caves,
where the temperature never rises above 31°F. Even if
you've already done some caving, you'll find this
attraction to be different. From Grants, the old road
continues as SR 122 through **Milan, Prewitt,** and
Thoreau (pronounced locally as *threw*) and across the
Continental Divide. Return to I-40 for just over ten
miles, then take the Iyanbito Exit and continue into
Gallup on the main thoroughfare, marked Highway 66.

More than most cities on the highway, Gallup
maintains a sense of the Route 66 era. Little has been
lost and, as the old alignment jogs south on First Street,
then west on Coal Avenue before returning to Highway
66, look for some of the fine old buildings like the
Drake and Grand hotels, and the El Morro Theater, also
designed by the Boller Brothers. Ask for the guide to
historic buildings when you arrive.

Gallup also has something few other places on
Route 66 can claim—a longtime Hollywood connection.
From *Redskin,* filmed in 1929, to the more recent
adventures of *Superman,* the Gallup area has provided
unequaled movie scenery. And El Rancho Hotel, now
beautifully and responsibly restored, was the on-location
home to stars like Tracy and Hepburn, Bogart,

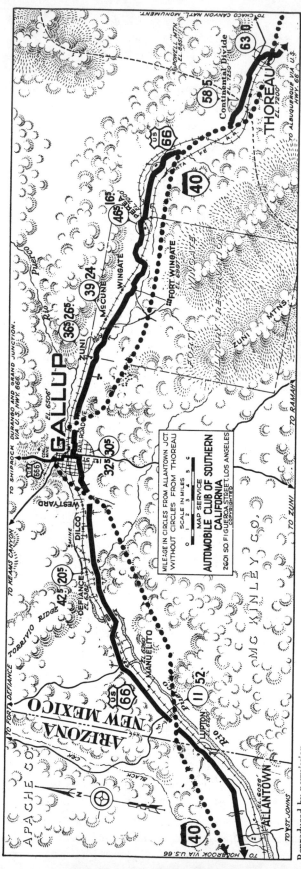

Hayworth, Flynn, and Peck. A production designer's dream, the hotel at first looks like an architectural collision between Mount Vernon and a backlot set for *Viva Villa.* There's even an Uncle Remus Wishing Well out front. Still, the overall effect is both inviting and absolutely right. How could it be otherwise? El Rancho, it has always been said, was designed for none other than R. E. Griffith, brother of the great film pioneer D. W. Griffith.

But hold the phone! There's a mystery brewing here. Exactly the kind of tale that the stars who stayed here, and movie fans everywhere, love. The truth is, D. W. Griffith *never had* a brother named R. E. Griffith. Those initials appear to belong instead to Raymond E. Griffith, a silent-film star turned comedy writer and producer.

R.E. had talent, no doubt about that, and was a production whiz, but he had another characteristic, too. He was known in the industry as a pathological teller of tales, often making up outlandish stories just to see if he could get away with it.

Or the obscure Mr. Griffith may have been another person altogether. But whatever his true identity, you've got to give the fellow credit. He put his D. W. Griffith story over on everyone for fifty years. So when you stay at El Rancho—and you simply must— drop by the taproom and hoist a glass to the memory of R. E. Griffith, who in death as in life damn near did fool all of the people all of the time.

To continue on the old road from Gallup, head directly west on Highway 66 and pass under I-40, remaining on the north side through **Mentmore.** This is a lovely section of old Route 66, well up and away from the interstate. Notice the old hand-turned silver and black guardrail posts in front of the church school a few miles out. And as the road reaches a high point along the south-facing bluffs, stop for a truly marvelous view of the entire valley—only part of what is denied the interstate traveler a few miles away. Also, take a moment to see how different are the westbound and eastbound views. It hardly looks like the same road.

Cross under I-40 to the south side as you near **Manuelito** and continue west toward the Arizona line.

For years a great arch, supported by Eiffel Towerish
strap-iron columns and topped by a large US 66 shield,
stood on the state border, wishing travelers well and
asking them to come again. Like so many other simple
things etched sharply in the common memory, the arch
is gone now. Hardly even a photograph remains. But
would it not be grand to create and preserve for all
those who will yet travel this road a new archway in
the same style? There is a sign at the border, of course.
But you pass *through* an arch and only go *by* a sign. It's
a different feeling, passing under an arch—a feeling far
more in tune with this old road and the way it conveys
us, more gently somehow, from one state to the next.

CHAPTER

7

Arizona

Arizona is one of the youngest states in the Union, last of the continental territories to be admitted, and one of the most thinly populated. But Arizona can take care of itself, thank you very much.

That's the view of many folks along the route through the upper part of the state. It's been a useful attitude to have around here, too. Poor relation to the sprawling developments of southern Arizona (itself too often a poor cousin to Southern California), the northern part of the state has learned to light its own lamp, carry its own bucket.

A lot of folks living close by old Route 66 are transplants from other orphan regions—the Ozarks of Missouri or the panhandles of Oklahoma and Texas—and they know how the government-and-commerce game works: *If you want to play ball, take the sprawl and all.* Nothing doing, the people of northern Arizona have replied. Good for them.

This is harsh but beautiful country, the air clear and sharp, unspoiled for the most part. Mountains like the San Francisco Peaks rise spectacularly from a flattened landscape, allowing you to watch them come closer for hours before the highway finally curves around their base near the junction with the main north-south road.

Cattle are raised in northern Arizona, but it is not feed-and-ship cattle country so much as it is the true Cowboy-and-Indian country of western legend. Zane Grey loved this land. He rode it and walked it and wrote about it. His was a special brand of romantic western—the kind where the hero still triumphs and rides through purple sage into a crimson sunset with his equally tough but tender sweetheart. Over the years, nearly a hundred and fifty million copies of Grey's books have been sold, with many made and remade into movies as well. So it is difficult to exaggerate the influence his notions of manhood, womanhood, and social justice have had on the American culture, and on anyone traveling old Route 66 across this land.

What's more, with the passage of only fifty years or so, the frontier is still very much a part of everything you'll find here. Stories of shoot-outs, lost gold mines, and desert massacres are still told by the people who lived through those days. It's a time warp worth stepping into.

There is also a compelling intimacy about the way old Route 66 and the land go on together. At night, especially, there is a personal feeling of timelessness here. Once you are away from the lights—east of Holbrook, up toward the Grand Canyon, or along the great northering loop west of Seligman—take time to stand for a while in the night. Pull the darkness around you like a cloak and feel what it is to be on the frontier of your own being, the land spilling away beyond your sight and hearing. Haul the stars down—so many here you may not even recognize old friends among them. Bring them close. Feel your own breathing and the life, unseen but sensed, everywhere around.

There are not many places left in which to take a moment like this. Arizona, along old Route 66, is one of the last.

Lupton to Flagstaff

Continuing on the south side of I-40, the old route passes through **Lupton,** on the border, and then recrosses to the north side for **Allentown, Houck, Sanders,** and **Chambers.** From Sanders to Chambers, the road on the north side is only partially paved with some gravel stretches and dead ends. Since the road largely disappears most of the way from Chambers to **Holbrook,** it is better to rejoin the interstate at Lupton.

Mostly, this is a section of lost towns: Houck, Cuerino, Navapache, and Goodwater. But about twenty miles beyond Chambers, keep watch for the Petrified Forest National Park and Painted Desert. Of these, the Petrified Forest is the more interesting, with a good deal of old Route 66 flavor remaining. Take Exit 311 and cross over I-40 southbound on the Park road, then continue westbound on US 180 (formerly US 260) into Holbrook on Hopi Boulevard, following Business Loop 40.

Watch for the Pow Wow Trading Post (really a wow with the neon lit up at night), plus Joe and Aggie's Cafe and a breakfast favorite, Gabrielle's Pancake House. If you've always wanted to sleep in a teepee ("Oh, puh-*leeze,* can't we?"), Holbrook is the best place in the West to do it. The design for Wigwam Village was patented in 1936, with the first units constructed in Kentucky and the Southeast. A similar teepee motel was also built on old Route 66 in Rialto, California, but only the Holbrook units have been completely renovated. Call ahead, though; the Holbrook wigwams are not always open.

Rejoin the interstate west of Holbrook. This was once a fairly touristy stretch of old Route 66 and some remnants like Geronimo's Trading Post still survive. Maybe you can skip the sand paintings, but can you really go home without a rubber tomahawk? There were some fine souvenir places on the old alignment through **Joseph City,** west of Business Loop 40, but these are

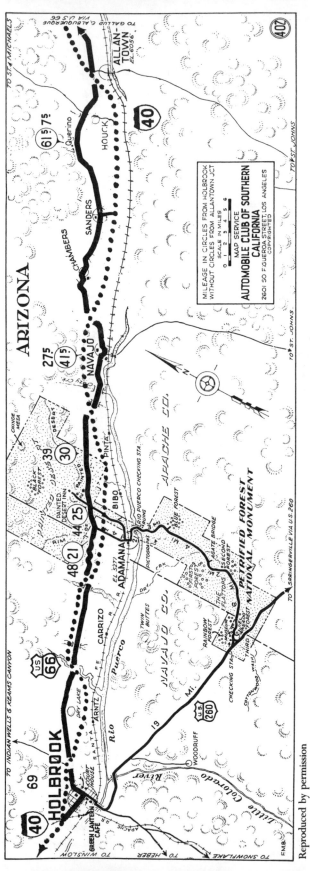

Reproduced by permission

empty or in ruin now. The Jackrabbit Trading Post hangs in there, though. All those yellow-and-black signs with the crouching rabbit that you've been seeing . . . Well, HERE IT IS!

Continuing on I-40 toward **Winslow,** watch for Hibbard Road (Exit 264). It's the beginning of a marvelous little section of old, old Route 66—a wonderful stretch to drive and photograph, with its solitary line of aged power poles. Marching bravely off by itself into the surrounding desert, this small remnant of the old road conveys a strong feeling of what it was like to make a great crossing in the 1930s and '40s. Take care, however; this section has not been well maintained.

Creviced arroyos, long sloping rifts, grassy hardpan all around. This western New Mexico–eastern Arizona region has a high-desert sweetness that can make you lightheaded with solitude. Sometimes, toward either end of a long driving day, a run through this country brings up an ancient German word, *fernweh.* It has no equivalent in English, but it represents a longing for, a need to return to, a place you've never been.

It's in the nature of a desert to be harsh. But here, on this old, old section of Route 66, there is a sense of poignance as well. If you've got a cassette player and a traveling tape collection, pull out a few tunes that bring you other voices, other times—that may even remind you of loves now gone separate ways—because this border region is special. Whether you are ambling along on the old road or slipping down the interstate, it's a stretch where you can see yourself more clearly, hear the past more sweetly.

Continuing on into town, just follow Business Loop 40. Second Street is the best-remembered of the older alignments, but after the one-way division, both current routes become part of US 66.

Winslow is often remembered for two things: national roadside marketing and interesting ladies. Roadies may improve their prospects locally by getting duded up a bit at the Store For Men before standing on a corner to wait for a girl (my lord) in a flatbed Ford. Eagles are nothing, you see, if not observant.

Like Meramec Caverns and the Jackrabbit,

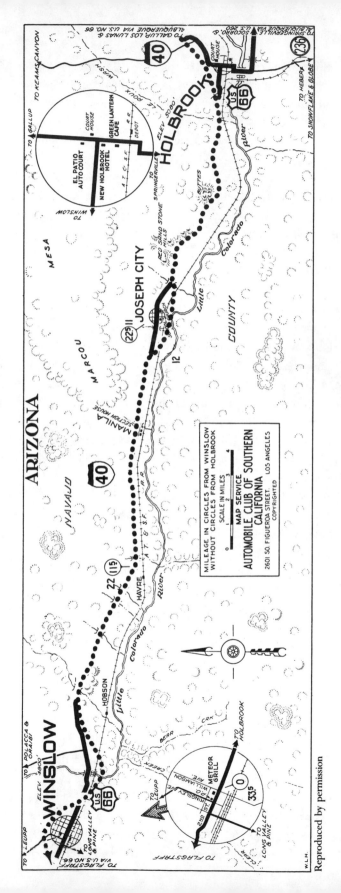

Reproduced by permission

Winslow's Store For Men was one of the pioneers in roadside advertising. Its signs wound up as far away as Paris and Guam. And Store For Men was one of the rule-breakers, too. It was generally believed that billboards and bumper stickers might bring in travelers the first time but would not generate many return visits. Roadside ads were considered one-shots. But the Jackrabbit and Store For Men signs—which almost always appeared together—practically wallowed in repeat business.

Currently, there's a renewed interest in old Route 66 in Winslow. Merchants are recognizing the high level of curiosity about the old route and restorations are underway. There are also a couple of interesting restaurants in town. At the east end of town, serving good food on Route 66 for thirty-five years, is the Falcon Restaurant. On the west end, it's the Entré. Plan to take a little time here.

Rejoin I-40 to the exit for Meteor Crater or continue on for a special stop at **Two Guns.** Here you'll find, spanning Diablo Canyon, an alignment of Route 66 so old that it shows little sign of ever having been paved.

Even better, for a buck or so, some good old boys at the present service station will direct you to the remains of an old last-chance gas stop, once featuring live but, sadly, caged mountain lions. If you step carefully among the ruins, it's possible to find the ticket window and main entrance to the old attraction. There are so many ghosts here, though, that even the newer junk takes on a timeworn character.

Do your best to visit this relic around sundown or at daybreak, when the shadows are deep and the wind-that-walks can be heard through the arroyos. At these times especially, there's no other spot along the old route with quite the feeling of the ruins at Two Guns. It's a perfect place to salute the past. And a last chance to say goodbye to one of the few reminders of a bygone institution of the American road in the West.

Signs for a last-chance, often crudely hand-lettered, told the whole story, made the entire pitch, in just a few words. In a time when neither travelers nor townies did a lot of reading, short copy was good copy.

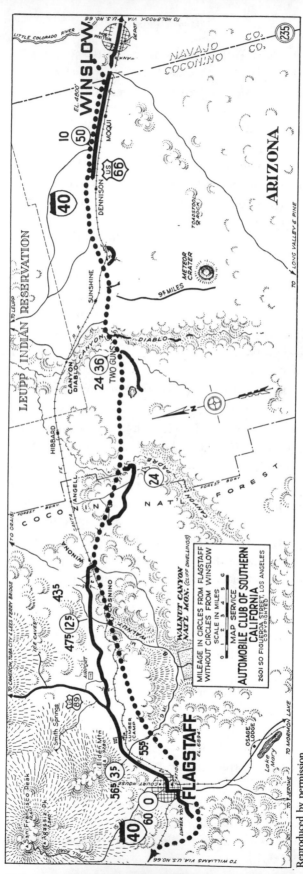

OPEN DESERT AHEAD . . . LAST CHANCE GAS AND
RATTLESNAKE RANCH . . . NO WATER—150 MILES . . . LAST
CHANCE FOR GAS . . . COLD DRINKS . . . SEE TWO-HEADED
RATTLER . . . EDUCATIONAL . . . EXCITING . . . LAST
CHANCE . . . RATTLESNAKES TURN HERE . . . A final sign,
usually on the far side of the last-chance, often
displayed only a skull and crossbones—leaving the rest
to your imagination.

Probably not half the backseat kids who wanted to
see the advertised exhibit ever got to do so. And
perhaps it's just as well. That way, most of us can
remember those old tourist traps more for what they
promised to be than for what they surely were. Rest in
peace, last-chance.

Heading for **Flagstaff,** take Bobby Troup's advice
and "don't forget **Winona.**" It's only a one-blink town,
but the folks at the little trading post are friendly and
helpful. It's also the gateway to an absolutely beautiful
drive along the old alignment, now nicely repaved, into
Flagstaff. Take the Camp Townsend/Winona Road exit,
continue to the junction with US 89, and then turn
south for town.

If you're planning a side trip to the Grand
Canyon, you may wish to turn north on US 89 instead.
Of the routes to either the South or North Rim, the
drive north on US 89 and west on SR 64 is perhaps the
most interesting. Or, if you prefer to duck into Flagstaff
first, take US 180 north to **Grand Canyon Village.**
When at the South Rim, it's well worth while to stay
or at least take a meal at El Tovar, a grand old lodge
at the canyon's edge that speaks eloquently of days gone
by. With Hopi House next door, the whole place
smacks of oatmeal for breakfast and daily constitu-
tionals. It's bully. Plan well in advance, however;
reservations can be difficult the year around.

If you will not be visiting Grand Canyon this time,
but still have a day to spend in the area, there's a
wonderful loop to the southwest through Oak Creek
Canyon and **Sedona** on US 89A. Then, jogging south
on SR 179, take a couple of hours at the unusual cliff
dwelling of Montezuma's Castle, an early Route 66
attraction still little changed. From **Camp Verde,**
return to US 89 via **Cottonwood.** Continue west and

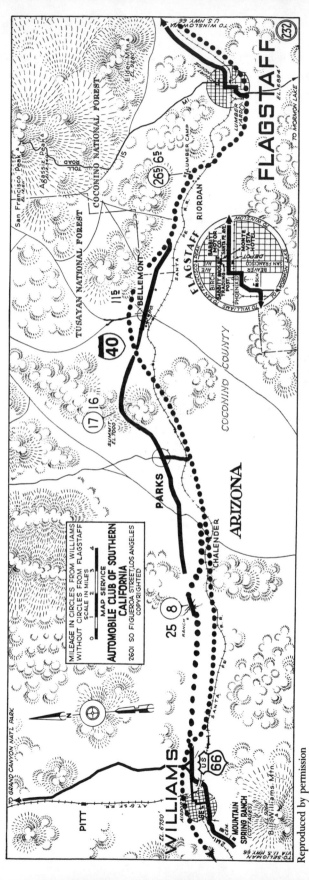

north through Chino Valley to I-40 just east of **Ash Fork.** In any case, by taking US 89 north or US 89A south, you will miss only a very little of the old alignment.

Flagstaff is a mixed bag of old Route 66 survivors and new construction, yet its motel row and businesses retain much of the old-road feeling—like the Santa Fe freights that grumble and growl just beyond your rented doorstep, to the delighted squeals of some, all through the night.

And new traditions are always forming. Some travelers are already calling the large Checkerboard building Fort Purina. One block west of the old railroad depot, turn south from Santa Fe Avenue, onto Beaver Street, west again on Phoenix Avenue, and then south on Milton Road (US 89).

As you drive through town, consider how all this might now look if Flagstaff had become the movie capital of the world. Because it almost did. A few years before Route 66 began service, a talented and extremely ambitious young man was steaming west on the Atchison, Topeka & Santa Fe. Folded in his coat pocket was a new screenplay, and in his mind's eye he could see every detail of how it would be made—in the real West, with real cowboys and Indians, under open skies. Fed up with Long Island studios where no one knew a cactus from a tin can, the young man was certain from his readings of Zane Grey that Flagstaff was the perfect location. The film he would make there would be grand, sweeping, magnificent—an *epic*.

It would also be wet, if he tried to make it in Flagstaff, where great, sodden flakes of snow were plopping softly into streams of icy mush along the platform as the train pulled in. For young Cecil B. DeMille, though, one look was enough. He never even left his Pullman, but went right on to Los Angeles, where he made the world's first feature-length film, *Squaw Man* (1914), using regular drugstore cowboys. But the incident must have left its mark on him, for through the monumental, biblical films DeMille later made, there always ran a theme of uncontrollable natural forces. And water, lots and lots of water.

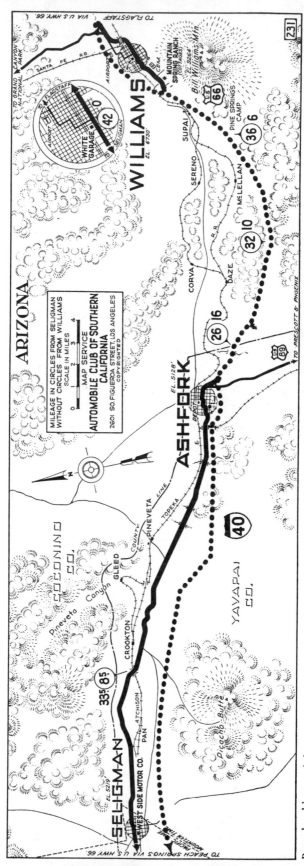

Flagstaff to Needles

Continue west on I-40. There is a short segment of old highway on the south side at **Bellemont,** but it is poorly surfaced and dead-ends after a couple of miles. For a very pretty forest drive on an old alignment, however, take Parks Road (Exit 178) to the north, turning west at the stop. Then, at Deer Farm Road, rejoin the interstate. Business loops follow the old route through **Williams.** A pair of very interesting tours (one for mountain bikes) has been developed by the U.S. Forest Service covering sections of nearby Route 66 now on the National Register. True roadies will want to pick up a brochure at the Chalender District office in Williams.

Although the long loop to the Colorado River begins at the Crookton Road Exit, you may wish to continue on the interstate until **Seligman,** since the old road between has been in a poor state of repair. Seligman was one of the earliest towns to support the movement to revitalize old Route 66. While there, pick up a brochure on this grand, 160-mile section of the old road prepared by the Historic Route 66 Association of Arizona.

Farther along, you'll find Grand Canyon Caverns, perhaps the only attraction in the West to survive at such a distance from any interstate exit. It's a good tour and, like the Missouri and New Mexico caves, has changed little with time. Then it's on to **Peach Springs** and Crozier Canyon, where the last unpaved section of old Route 66 remained until the late 1930s. At **Truxton,** try the Frontier Cafe. The coffee's good, the food is some of the best anywhere along the route —and the stories are on the house.

Finally, down a twenty-mile straight, **Kingman** comes into sight. After sundown, it's like being on a long final approach—more like landing than driving into town. Along Andy Devine Avenue, there are a few survivors like El Trovatore, and the Brandin' Iron Motel

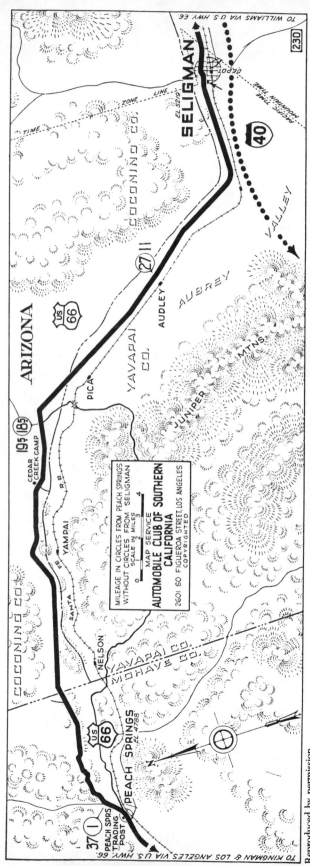

Reproduced by permission

with a flickering neon sign that usually reads BRA IN. On past the newer Route 66 Distillery, there's the old Santa Fe depot, done in Mission Revival style and hoping for restoration. In between, on the right, is a three-star pizza joint called Angel's. If you're a confirmed divie and constantly on the lookout for that special good-food dump, Angel's is as unpretentious as they come.

An excellent minitour of Kingman's more-interesting buildings has been organized by the local historical society, which also maintains a fine little museum connected to the Kingman Chamber of Commerce at the Y on the west end of town. If your itch for history runs a little deeper, take some time for the old wagon wheel tracks at the base of White Cliffs. A brochure is available at the museum.

Departing Kingman, continue on the old route through a deep cut to the **McConnico** undercrossing. At the stop, turn west under the interstate and follow Oatman Road—the last and best part of the western Arizona section of old Route 66.

Be forewarned, however. If you are a longtime flatlander or are driving an RV that handles about like the Graf Zeppelin in a high wind, you may want to take the interstate and continue your tour of old Route 66 in Needles. Otherwise, precautions noted, carry on.

If a major part of your driving time until now has been up on the superslab, you'll be surprised how quickly civilization fades once you are away from town. There are real beginnings and endings here on old Route 66, and a truer sense of being alone, dependent on your vehicle and the road itself to take you safely through Along this stretch especially, there's often the very first glimmer of how it must have been for travelers forty or fifty years ago. As you roll deeper into the desert, a more primitive part of the brain begins to stir. You may find yourself listening more carefully to the engine, checking the gauges, feeling with your hands what's happening on the road just below. By the time you reach **Cool Springs Camp** (which is none of those, but only a trashed ruin now) you may even have heard some mechanical notes never audible to you

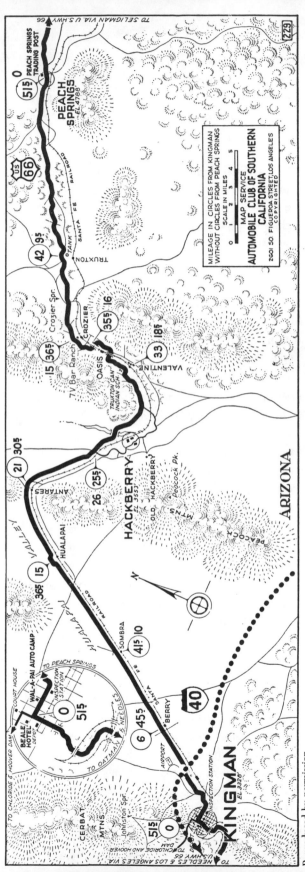

Reproduced by permission

before. Funny how perfectly good engines can sound rough way out here.

Up to this point, where the grade begins in earnest, your main concern will be the odd jackrabbit or roadrunner grown unused to traffic. But you can soon expect other road companions. Wild burros, brought here by prospectors long ago and turned loose, now number in the thousands. They also blend so well into the desert scrub that it is difficult to see them before they saunter onto the road to inspect you. Protected by the Wild Horse Act, they are not timid. And if you pull over for a moment to take in the view, you may hear them calling to one another—announcing your arrival perhaps. For they are born tourist hustlers with an acquired taste for the junk food we are known always to have with us.

This segment of old Route 66 is also just the ticket for drivers or riders with an affinity for switchbacks. And if you fancy yourself something of a canyon buster, the run over Sitgreaves Pass into Oatman may be just what you've been waiting for. Especially if you've dreamed of the twisties on the famous Stelvio Road in the Alps, but cannot yet make the fare to Europe.

All right, then, just imagine an alpine road dropped down into the middle of the American desert. Instead of black ice and maniacal Italian bus drivers, here you'll be dealing with scattered patches of shoulder gravel, rockhounds in 4 × 4s, and the occasional band of wide-angle choppers. Still, it's often said that the highway surface, curves, and gradients are a miniature version of the Stelvio run.

In the old days, when cars and trucks had little power, even in first gear, the only way up the 3,500-foot grade from Oatman east was in reverse—a craft mastered so well by locals that they could do it at top speed, by rearview mirror only, while dangling one arm loosely out the window. So, as you drive these marvelous old switchbacks, imagine how city-bred easterners must have felt when they veered into a blind, cliff-hugging curve, only to encounter some mad local coming full steam up the mountain *backward*.

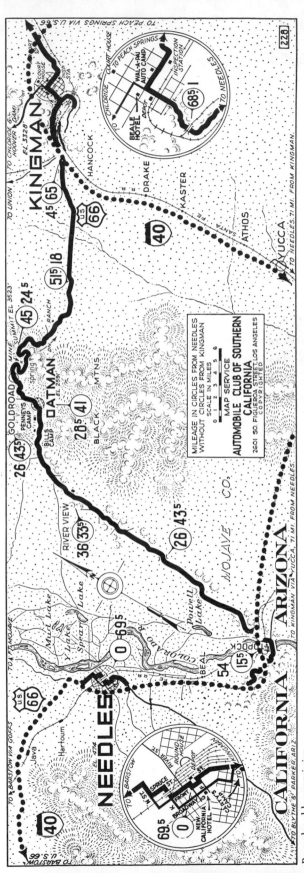

Commercial laundries at the bottom of the hill must
have done a hell of a business.

Switchbacks still ahead for the moment, continue
on to **Ed's Camp** (which is both) a few miles short of
Sitgreaves Pass. As you'll quickly notice, Ed's is more
than a way station for the overheated and overfed
traveler. It's also a desert-style flea market with all sorts
of collectible debris lying in wait for those with a skosh
more room in the back.

Just over the summit, you'll also discover the
earthly remains of **Goldroad.** Just a few adobe walls
and stone foundations are here now, the owners having
decided to save on their taxes by burning the town to
the ground. So much for architectural and cultural
heritage.

Once at the center of rich finds, this entire area
had already been fairly well picked over by prospectors
when one José Jerez discovered a major new
outcropping. The town boomed again as everyone
cashed in on the find. Everyone but José, that is, who
spent his small share and then walked out by the road
one night, sat down, and chugalugged a bottle of rat
poison. *C'est la prospérité.*

Down in **Oatman,** a few minutes past the final
switchbacks, the main street is a curious jam-up of gun-
toting locals, hand-holding teens, and camera-ridden
tourists. Plus, of course, the omnipresent burros who
happily join in the game of hustling all the out-of-
towners. Take a while to explore the character of this
place that, booming or broke, has always gone its own
way. And be sure to look in on the Oatman Hotel.
Although it's on the National Register, the place is
better known as the honeymoon hideaway of Clark
Gable and Carole Lombard.

Before leaving Oatman, check on road conditions
south to **Topock.** The chuckholes on that stretch can
be downright malevolent. So, unless the road has
recently been repaved, head straight west at the Y
beyond town, turn south on SR 95, and cross the back-
door bridge into Needles, or continue south to Topock
and rejoin I-40 westbound into California. If it's
anytime around summer, you'll know why the Joads

walked out into the Colorado River shallows and just stood there after driving this stretch. The road from Oatman to Topock can be as tough as any road ever gets.

CHAPTER

8

California

Crossing into California isn't the adventure it once was. But neither is it the terror.

Back in the Dust Bowl days there were barricades out on the road. Armed men, too—local recruits mostly— many hired from the worst of the saloons along the highway. Men itching to call out anyone they didn't know, shoot anything that moved, club anyone who might resist. California was terrified, all right. Frightened silly that this stirred-up cloud of people would discover that it could be an army. An army that could take the whole state if it wanted. And right here, close to the border, is where that fear showed most.

A man with a Sam Browne belt and heavy, rib-kicking boots would be looking down the long, ragged line of overloaded, steaming jalopies. Peering into the first car. Studying some patient, fumbling man at the wheel, the enduring but crumpled face of his wife, and the sit-still-now looks of the children, their eyes shifting from the glinting badge to the black billy club now in momentary repose at the open side window.

You folks planning to cross? Stupid question. What would they be doing in line for near a day, if they didn't intend to cross? But barricades and shotguns are the tools of men who are themselves desperate in some way. Intelligence is rarely deputized.

You folks got any money? Uh-huh. How much? Let me see it. The money is produced. There isn't a lot, even by Okie standards, but it's something. A little change, a few sweat-soaked bills folded into a waistband pocket still stretched from the watch it no longer holds. The driver sneaks a quick glance back over his shoulder at the family in the next car down the line, fearing that he is somehow holding them up.

Looking more carefully at the kids now. Any sign of disease? Any excuse at all to turn the car back, send these people off to some other border? But there is no reason. Thinking of his own family, perhaps, the man with the badge steps back and without expression waves the car on.

But before he is out of second gear, the freed driver can see in his mirror that the car behind has already been turned away and out of line. Sent back to Arizona or somewhere else. Sent to anywhere-but-here. For some reason. For any reason . . .

Everything has changed since then, of course. Or it has seemed to. The agricultural inspection station was even moved some years back. Crossing into California is no longer a problem, unless you happen to be an inveterate apple-snacker or cactus-collector. And, thanks to equal opportunity, some of the agricultural inspectors are more than pleasant; they are lovely. A nice touch. A bit of tinseltown, way out here on the desert.

Few travelers think of the desert as being the *real* California, though. Not the California of laid-back surfers, iron-kneed skateboarders, and delectable beach bunnies. That California still lies well to the west. The desert here is a harsh, tough place. A place where the well-watered California dream has not yet made its mark. The other California is closer to the sea, where life is easier, where both cars and humans seem to endure forever.

At a traditional picnic held in Los Angeles by emigrants from Iowa, some have been heard to say that California is a crazy place. Perhaps that's so. Perhaps all those people from Iowa are being held captive out here, without anyone's knowledge. Perhaps, as someone also suggested, the continent has tilted so that everything not screwed tightly down comes sliding right into Southern California. If that's true, it has produced a wondrous blend.

So welcome to California. Spiritual home of the Sing-Along *Messiah*. Birth state of right-turn-on-red.

It's an interesting place.

Needles to San Bernardino

Some regular desert travelers believe **Needles** was named for the prickly desert heat. Not true, though. The town was named for the spiky mountains to the south, beyond the graceful, silver-arched bridge over the Colorado River. That same bridge, by the way, once carried old Route 66 and still serves as a pipeline support. Notice also that from Needles west, there are over a hundred miles of open desert with few services before Barstow, so you may want to see to your vehicle's fluids and your own before heading out.

For the city portion of old Route 66 through Needles, take the third exit (US 95) northbound after crossing the river and continue through town on Broadway. Watch for the 66 and Palm motels and the once-magnificent El Garces, formerly a Fred Harvey hotel, now only an appendage of the Amtrak station. For breakfast, the Hungry Bear Restaurant, next to the Travelodge near the west end of town, specializes in homemade biscuits and gravy and is frequented by many locals.

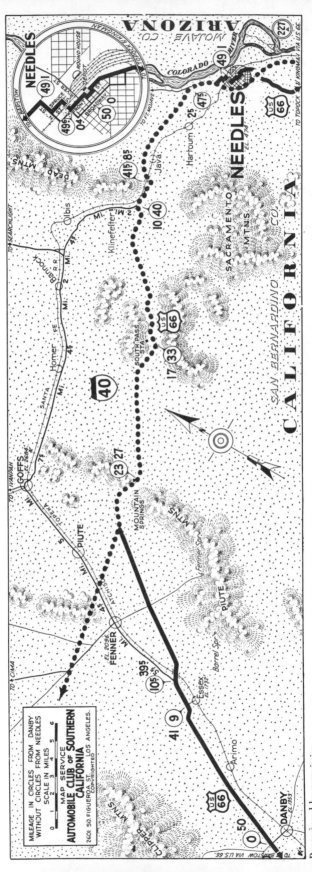

Beyond Needles, return to I-40 and exit at US 95 for a forty-mile segment of the old route that ran through **Goffs** until 1931. An interesting, crusty desert town, Goffs is a survivor in its own right—one of those places that wouldn't know how to give up. Once, because it is usually at least fifteen degrees cooler than Needles, Goffs was a regular little summer resort. Now, even with double bypass surgery and air conditioning everywhere on the desert, the town carries on somehow. Good place for a soda and a chat.

To continue on the old route, cross under I-40 near **Fenner.** You'll be on a well-known section posted as National Old Trails, of which this highway was a part before becoming Route 66. Rolling on toward **Essex,** though, keep a lookout ahead. Just a few miles beyond the interstate exit, where the road curves down and away to the right, you'll get a first look at what lay in wait for the pioneer or the Dust Bowl family. Imagine the feeling: just when you have struggled past the terrible grade west of Needles and believe the worst to be over, you see what must yet be endured.

Out beyond the shimmering, glass-hard desert floor in front of you is another range of mountains, a thousand feet higher than those you just crossed. And beyond them yet another great barrier range, higher still. Peaks to 10,000 feet, some still carrying the snows of winter. Perhaps you tremble a little at the thought of what it will be like to go on. Most did tremble. And some, taking in the seeming endlessness of these trials, just stopped their creaking wagons or steaming old cars and without a word to anyone, walked away into the desert and disappeared. It was not a good end. But it was a way to have it over with, and that's all some could find for themselves in this merciless place. Just an end to it all.

On toward **Chambless,** though, the desert takes on a different meaning. Nearly fifty years ago, the desert here meant not death but a chance at life. It was during World War II and a very bad time for America, just then. General Erwin Rommel, Hitler's Desert Fox, was loose with his Panzer Corps, racing almost unopposed across North Africa toward the unlimited supply of oil needed by the Nazi war machine. If we could not

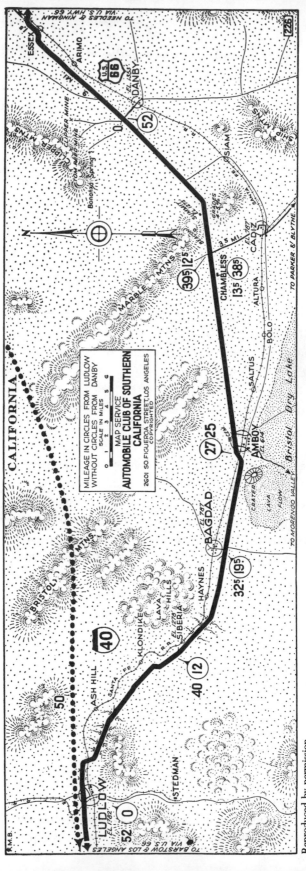

support the beleaguered British there soon, the war would most certainly be lost.

Enter the singular General George S. Patton, "Old Blood-and-Guts" himself. Patton had been reared in this part of California and knew that the Mojave was not only similar to North Africa, it could be worse. So he pressed every tank, truck, motorcycle, and reconnaissance aircraft he could find into service as part of his Desert Training Center. Over two million men were trained to survive in the ten thousand square miles of desert surrounding you now. In the end, the Great Mojave did its job. And Patton and the Second Corps did theirs, sweeping through North Africa as if they knew their way around—with no surprises their own desert hadn't already shown them.

Now the Mojave is quiet again, a place for reflection. A mile or so beyond **Amboy** and a few yards to the south is Amboy Crater. If you're due for a stretch about now and you've not visited an extinct volcano, it's certainly worth the short walk up to the cone.

Halfway from Amboy to **Siberia** lies sleepy **Bagdad,** location for the film *Bagdad Café,* which you may later want to buy or rent on videocassette. It is a marvelous tale of human relationships and what kind of endurance and personal responsibility it takes to transform misgivings and self-pity into trust and love. As they do in real life, the road and the desert strip away all but the essentials. Old Route 66 offers a way in and a way out. Everyone is free to choose either direction, with the desert burning away everything else. You may enjoy the movie or, funny as it is, you may find it distressing. Either way, you'll not soon forget it —or this stretch of highway.

A break in the old road occurs at **Ludlow.** To continue on Route 66, cross under I-40, head west over a newer service road, and then cross over the interstate and rejoin the old highway at **Lavic** for a short run to **Newberry Springs.** Recross to the north side of I-40 there, and continue on through **Minneola** and **Coolwater.**

Daggett, now an aging bridesmaid among railroad towns, was once a major transshipment point for the

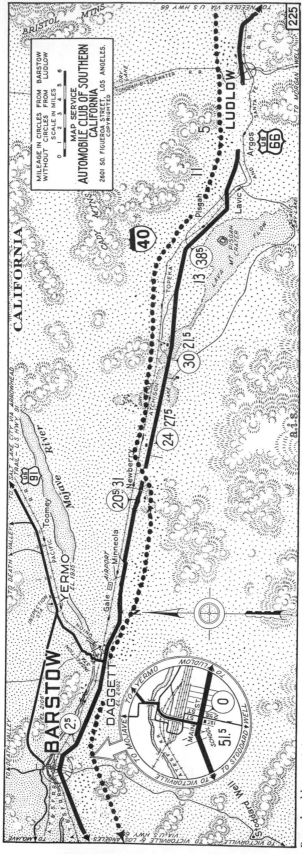

borax trade (Remember Ronald Reagan hosting *Death Valley Days?*) from **Calico** to the north. Fat and sassy, Daggett developers of the day were delighted to learn that the Santa Fe Railway planned to locate a major railroad complex in Daggett. But the price of land in the town was soon driven so high that discouraged Santa Fe officials built their complex farther on down the line at Waterman Junction, a nothing place at the time. Later, the junction was given the middle name of the then president of the railroad, William Barstow Strong. Downtown Daggett now has little more than a homey general store and the Stone Hotel, which the town is working to restore. The old Stone was a favorite hangout for Death Valley Scotty, Tom Mix, and Wallace Beery. It is not known, however, if they came here to tank up or dry out.

Just west of Daggett, old Route 66 passes through a Marine Corps depot. The east gate is not often open, though, so it's best to rejoin the interstate into **Barstow.** I-40 ends here, with I-15 continuing on toward San Bernardino.

Main Street in Barstow is old Route 66, so take that exit to continue west through **Lenwood**, **Hodge**, **Helendale,** and **Oro Grande.** It's an easy drive of thirty-eight miles or so on a well-maintained highway. Scenery is mixed: some high desert, some river basin. There'll be plenty of time to speculate on businesses like Honolulu Jim's that once populated this part of the route so long ago. How did the owner happen upon the name? Had he been a sailor stationed at Pearl Harbor? Or, like others in the tourist business along old Route 66, was he simply a master marketer? Ah, Honolulu Jim's. How does it manage to sound so wholesome, yet still carry a slight tinge of something just a bit illicit? Who could resist stopping for a cold ice cream soda, a chocolate malt, and perhaps a lei?

The old route crosses under I-15 to enter **Victorville,** where Main Street to Seventh Street was the alignment through town. Dyed-in-the-wool tourists and borderline necrophiles will surely want to visit Trigger, the stuffed horse—undoubtedly Roy Rogers's vision of equine immortality. Otherwise, you may want to keep on going.

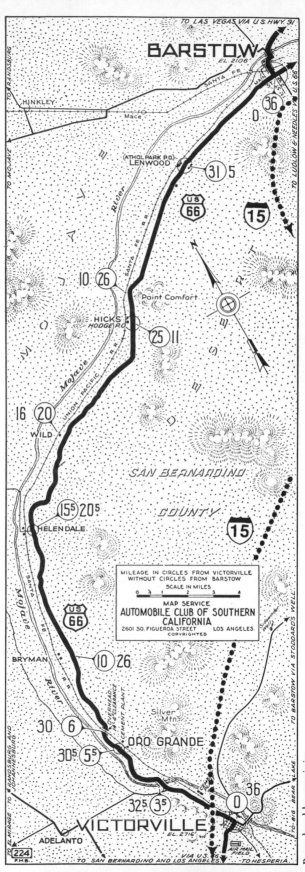

Reproduced by permission

From Victorville to San Bernardino (San Berdoo to locals), nearly all the old route lies directly beneath I-15. All, that is, except for a five-mile section that has a wonderful feeling of time suspended. Used by locals, this brief stretch turns up on the east side at the exit just beyond SR 138 at **Cajon Junction.** Twisting along below the newer highway, this old remnant follows the river wash and the Santa Fe tracks southeast to Cajon Mountain where you must rejoin I-15. If you've not had time for the longer loops through Goffs or Amboy or Helendale, be sure to take a few minutes for this brief interlude. If anyone ever films *Twilight Zone Meets Son of Route 66,* this piece of road is where it will be shot.

Also, if you have the time and have not visited Lake Arrowhead before, you may wish to exit a little earlier and take SR 138 and 189 over to **Arrowhead Village.** It's a lovely alpine setting and a soothing place to spend a night as you make the transition between the desert and Los Angelopolis.

At the **Devore** exit, you may follow old Route 66 again along Cajon Boulevard and southbound Mt. Vernon Avenue, but there is little sense of the old road remaining. A more convenient route is to exit at 5th Street, which flows into Foothill Boulevard (SR 66) and the old route.

San Bernardino to Santa Monica

A city in cultural transition, **San Bernardino** has often found itself trapped between two opposing mentalities. On one side is the kind of thinking that led city officials to burn down a landmark Route 66 motel on Mt. Vernon Avenue—just so the fire department could have some practice on a slow day. On the other side (most fortunately) is a civic heritage movement, which among other projects, guided the restoration of the famous California Theater. Located at 562 West 4th Street, adjacent to the old route, the California was designed by John Paxton Perrine and completed in 1928.

In those days, movie palaces commonly employed vaudeville acts to draw a larger audience, and the California was a major break-in theater for new talent. When sneak previews became common in the 1930s, the Santa Fe Railway became a virtual commuter line for all the stars who trekked out from Hollywood to San Bernardino to find glory or disaster in the first public showing of their latest films.

Will Rogers's last public appearance was at the California in 1935. Will headlined a star-filled benefit performance, featuring everyone from Buster Crabbe and Jane Withers, to unknowns like Rita Cansino, who would be later recognized as Rita Hayworth. Less than two months later Will was gone, killed in a plane crash on Alaska's North Slope with his pilot and good friend, Wiley Post. But the theater is still here, fully restored (now air conditioned, too) and rich with the original voice of its great Wurlitzer pipe organ. And thanks to local support, there's usually a good show on stage. So, if you're a little jaded from driving the desert, plan to spend the night here and take in a live performance. Most shows are not expensive, and it's a grand place to breathe in a moment from Southern California's golden past.

Crossing the Los Angeles basin could easily consume two days, if you take time to see everything along the route. There are also eighty miles of city streets and freeways between you and the Pacific Ocean, so you will want to avoid the jam-ups that occur between seven and ten in the morning and from four to seven on weekday afternoons. Mondays aren't so bad, but Murphy's Law rules supreme on Fridays.

If you are eager to complete your journey and simply want to get to the end of the old route in Santa Monica, it's easiest to take I-10 from San Bernardino all the way to the coast. Once in Santa Monica, exit on northbound Lincoln Boulevard, turn west again on Santa Monica Boulevard, and continue the few blocks to Ocean Avenue, where the old route ended. It's an easy freeway route to follow and, in moderate traffic, you can be there in about two hours.

With a half day or more, there is a nice combination route to follow that will keep you on the

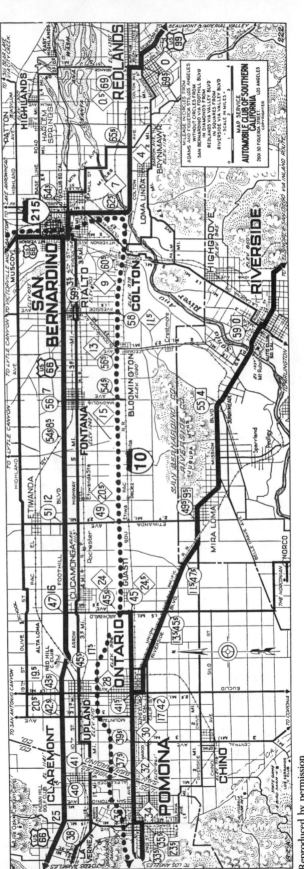

old alignment most of the way with least difficulty. From San Bernardino, continue west along Foothill Boulevard (SR 66). Just east of Pepper Avenue is the site of the twin to Holbrook's Wigwam Village. The property has been put up for sale, however, and its future is doubtful.

Although settlement of this region in Southern California stems directly from cultivation of the first orange groves and vineyards in the state, nearly all of that milk-and-honey life is gone now—replaced by a drive toward security rather than quality of life as the prime consideration. Huge, lighted signs on outsized buildings along this stretch carry martial nouns like SENTINEL, FORTRESS, and GUARDIAN, which appear with the same frequency as the word *Acme* once did in Warner Brothers cartoons. Now and then a light, earthy noun like SPRINGTIME pops up. But not often.

If you recall the running Jack Benny gag about a train that went through "An-a-heim, Azu-za, and Coook-a-monga," you're in luck. **Rancho Cucamonga** is next along the route. The old Virginia Dare Winery is one of California's oldest. Although not restored, it was at least rehabbed as part of a shopping center on the north side at Haven Avenue.

At Archibald Avenue, there is a gas station dating from the 1920s. And farther along, you'll find Dolly's Diner, serving hash-browns since 1944. The Sycamore Inn—a very special place and once a Butterfield Stage stop—has been offering good food and friendly service for over 140 years. If it's getting close on to suppertime, be sure to make a stop. Just as interesting and inviting in its own curio style is the Magic Lamp— catty-corner across the street.

In **Upland,** at Euclid Avenue, a statue of Madonna of the Trail (no relation to the star-crossed singer) marks the end of National Old Trails and stands as a tribute to the pioneer women of the westering movement. Also, if you are any kind of aviation buff, one of the finest collections in the West of vintage aircraft is displayed at the Planes of Fame Museum (best call for hours) adjoining the airport in **Chino,** about four miles south on Euclid. This field is home to a number of internationally known airshow/racing pilots and collectors, so there can be interesting traffic in the landing pattern on most any day.

Approaching **Glendora,** you'll have a choice of routes. For the older and more interesting 1930s alignment, turn north on Amelia Avenue and then west again on a somewhat displaced Foothill Boulevard. Some of these main-street buildings haven't changed in a hundred years, which is what the good people of Glendora intended. Jog south again on Citrus Avenue to join the newer Alosta Avenue alignment, and continue west.

In **Monrovia,** jog north on Shamrock Avenue, turning west on another section of Foothill Boulevard. Four blocks west of Myrtle Avenue, notice the famous Aztec Hotel, designed by Robert Stacy-Judd in 1926 as an all-out tourist grabber. Then, for a brief, mind-unbending side trip and a lovely lunchtime stroll, turn south on Baldwin Avenue for a visit to the Lucky Baldwin estate, now the Los Angeles Arboretum. You'll recognize the Queen Anne Cottage ("deh plane, deh plane") from the TV series *Fantasy Island*.

Jog south as Foothill enters **Pasadena,** and continue west. You're now on the Rose Parade route, so you might not want to try this on New Year's Day —unless New Year's happens to fall on a Sunday. Why? Because this is also genteel Pasadena where, in an age-old deal with local churches, the Tournament of Roses committee agreed never to do it on Sunday. Why? Too immoral? No, parishioners were concerned that the parade might have frightened the horses tied up during services. Parade or no, take time for architectural and museum tours here if at all possible. Much can be found that is truly extraordinary.

Near Fair Oaks Avenue, the alignments of old Route 66 divide. An early version turned south on Fair Oaks, following Huntington Drive and North Broadway into downtown **Los Angeles**—past once-famous Ptomaine Tommy's restaurant, where the Chili Size was invented back during the Great Depression. Another routing continued west on Colorado Boulevard to Eagle Rock, where it turned south toward the central L.A. district.

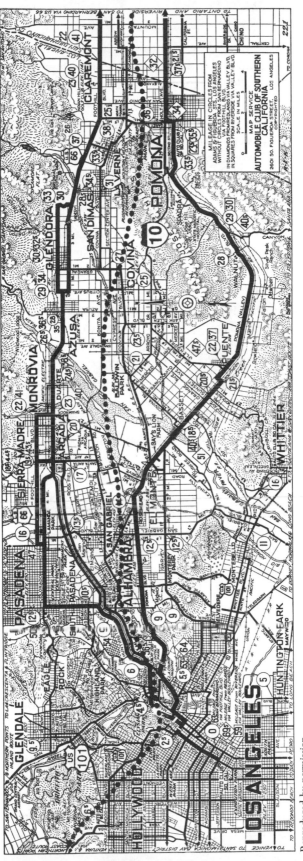

Neither of these routes has much to recommend it though, now that Tommy's is gone. It's better to take the newer alignment, which turns south on Arroyo Seco Parkway (SR 11 and 110). In 1941, the parkway became the world's first freeway and is now showing its age, so take care near the on-ramps where drivers must enter traffic at very low speeds. Follow the Arroyo Seco/Pasadena Freeway to the downtown interchange in Los Angeles. If time is short, change over to the Hollywood Freeway (US 101 and SR 2), also part of Route 66, and continue northwest to the Santa Monica Boulevard exit.

To follow an interesting 1930s alignment, however, take the exit leading to westbound Sunset Boulevard. Looming just a block south at Glendale Boulevard is the famous Angelus Temple built by Aimee Semple McPherson. Probably no one soared to quite the evangelistic heights reached by Sister Aimee, whose charisma and career survived publicized divorces, a self-described kidnapping of epic proportions, and dozens of simultaneous lawsuits. By 1941, the temple itself had become a prime tourist attraction along old Route 66.

Continue on Sunset and turn west on Santa Monica Boulevard. Above you, along here, is the famous HOLLYWOOD sign. Imported as a name from a Chicago suburb, the name was originally Hollywoodland, a real estate development west of Griffith Park. A landmark for motorists, pilots, and the starry-eyed, the sign has stood through thick and thin. With maintenance first discontinued in 1939, the sign has survived vandals, petty bureaucrats, destructive Santa Ana winds, and the stigma added by an actress's high dive from the top of the first letter to her death below. Now, with the LAND portion gone, the sign has been repaired and remains a beacon for a city that has officially never existed.

Continue west on Santa Monica Boulevard, through the boutique and little-theater district and past Barney's Beanery. If you liked Mort's Roadhouse in Glenarm, Illinois, you'll love Barney's.

Near the western boundary of **Beverly Hills,** seven blocks beyond Beverly Drive on Walden, is an architectural treat for fans of the silent-movie period. It's the Spadena house, a delightful Hansel and Gretel cottage designed by Henry Oliver in 1921. Originally, it

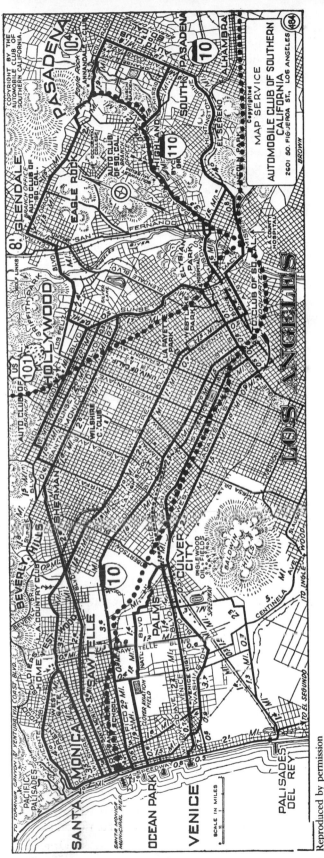

was the office of Irvin C. Willat Productions in Culver City, before being moved to its present site on the southeast corner of Carmelita. In late afternoon light, you can practically smell the gingerbread baking.

Farther along is glistening **Century City,** constructed by Alcoa in a flukish deal on the Twentieth Century–Fox backlot. Since a new Mercedes is common carriage here, the area is known chiefly for its upscale work ethic—you are even less what you drive than where you park—and for Harry's Bar and American Grill across from the Century Plaza Hotel.

Harry's is very dark and very good. It's also where they hold a well-known annual contest to see who can write most like Ernest Hemingway . . . *In the hazy, brown light of afternoon we would go to Harry's to do the watching and the writing. Tight-breasted waitresses would smile at us as they walked by. They had the long legs and full calves of dancers, which was their true profession, and we always smiled back. After a while, we would forget about the writing and just do the watching* . . . Some say the contest affects everybody.

After you're done with whatever you decide to do at Harry's, though, continue on through West Los Angeles on the old route toward **Santa Monica.**

The City of Santa Monica is spiritually as well as politically separate from Los Angeles. It begins officially at Centinela Avenue and ends at the ocean tideline. For a short time, very late in life, Route 66 was shunted several blocks south. But that alignment has never been, to travelers and fans, the true highway. Most prefer to remember old Route 66 on Santa Monica Boulevard, where it had been since 1935. Only a few more blocks to go now. Then, it's Ocean Avenue, at last—and the old highway simply ends.

The Belle Vue Restaurant, right on the corner, has a cozy, publike atmosphere if you're in a celebrative mood. Straight across the street are the Palisades, above Pacific Coast Highway. To the south a few blocks is Santa Monica Pier. If you're a Redford and Newman fan, you'll want to take a ride on the beautifully restored carousel—it's the one used in George Roy Hill's 1973 film *The Sting.*

Just west of the intersection a few feet is a plaque memorializing Route 66 as Will Rogers Highway. Actually, the plaque has more to do with promotion of the 1952 film *The Story of Will Rogers,* starring Will Rogers, Jr., since the highway itself had been named for Will Rogers nearly fifteen years earlier. If you're observant, you may even have seen a highway marker announcing such in John Ford's production of *The Grapes of Wrath,* released in 1940.

Before leaving this area, however, be sure to make a pilgrimage to Will Rogers's ranch, now preserved with the cooperation of the Rogers family as a California state park. Drive northwest on Ocean Avenue three blocks and, at California Avenue, turn left and head down the hill to Pacific Coast Highway. Continue on PCH a little over three miles, turn right onto Sunset Boulevard (yes, it's the same one), and wind inland to number 14253, on the left. Signs will guide you up to the ranch itself. Or, most anyone you meet on horseback will gladly direct you.

There's more of a feeling of Will himself—what he loved and what enriched the caring he felt for all of us—here on this lovely 185-acre spread than you'll find anywhere else. Will's little office, where he did most of his writing, is just upstairs. In the early morning, with a light coastal fog hanging in the eucalyptus trees, you can practically feel the words coming through the window and down into his old typewriter.

Wiley Post used to sideslip his new monoplane in from the southeast, over the polo field, to land deftly on the wide, sloping lawn next to the house. Bring a lunch—you can picnic right on Wiley's runway. The whole place is truly inspiring, and you'll enjoy just wandering about on your own. In spring, when all the flowers bordering the old, board-and-batten ranch house are in bloom, it's a reminder that paradise is not somewhere up, up, and away. It's right here, all around. Some places just help us see it a little more clearly. Will Rogers's ranch is one of them.

Before going off to do any sightseeing, though, take time to stroll along the bluffs here in Santa Monica, as a way of completing your journey over old

Route 66. Watch the people. Breathe in some fresh sea air before the city gets hold of it.

Like most travelers who come to Southern California, you may not have exactly arrived. But the sea, the people, and Palisades Park all let you know that you are here.

You are definitely here.

OTHER ROADSIDE
Resources

Books

Route 66: The Mother Road, by Michael Wallis. St. Martin's Press, 1990. Carefully researched, warmly written. Lots of color photography. The definitive work on the life and times of US 66.

Route 66: The Highway and Its People, by Quinta Scott and Susan Croce Kelly. University of Oklahoma Press, 1988. Extensive collection of large-format black and white photographs supported by detailed firsthand accounts of roadside life on Route 66 in its heyday.

Route Sixty-Six Revisited: A Wanderer's Guide to New Mexico, by K. Hilleson. D. Nakii Enterprises, 1988. Wonderful source for folk tales, stories, and legends of the old route from Albuquerque to the Arizona border.

Route 66: Remnants, by Patricia R. Buckley. Self-published, 1988. Good vest-pocket history of the highway and how it came to be. Reliable source for information on various alignments

Roadfood and Goodfood, by Jane and Michael Stern. Alfred A. Knopf, 1986. This two-for-one guide to the pleasures of roadside dining remains the most entertaining as well as most helpful book of its kind. If you're fed up with plastic fare and a devotee of real cooking in all its forms, keep this book next to the Gideon in your motel room.

The Verse by the Side of the Road, by Frank Rowsome, Jr.
E. P. Dutton, 1966. Penultimate collection of the
Burma-Shave jingles, with a folksy history of the famous
signs. Did you know that every state had Burma-Shave
signs save Arizona, Nevada, and New Mexico?

A Guide Book to Highway 66, by Jack D. Rittenhouse.
Self-published, 1946. Now available in a facsimile
edition from University of New Mexico Press. The
granddaddy of all Route 66 books and as useful as it
ever was. Want to know if the Palace Hotel in Winslow
is a survivor from the old days on the highway? Jack's
book can tell you.

Tapes

"The Mother Road," performed by writer-singer Kevin
Welch, is the first new Route 66 song in thirty years or
more. The lyrics are sweet and the production work by
Paul Worley and Ed Seay is excellent. The album is
Kevin Welch, available on the Reprise label from Warner
Records.

Route 66, produced by Bob Burwell and directed by
Mike Merriman for Piper Productions. Music video
released in 1990 for Michael Martin Murphey's version
of Bobby Troup's "(Get Your Kicks on) Route 66,"
from Michael's album *Land of Enchantment* on Warner
Records.

Route 66: The Mother Road, produced by Nikki and Davia
Nelson. One-hour audiocassette available from National
Public Radio. Engaging storytelling style and interviews.
Just the thing to pop into the cassette player your first
day out. Phone: (800) 235–8273.

Going Somewhere: The Story of Route 66, produced by
Richard O. Moore. Originally a one-hour presentation,
this thirty-minute version is clearer and less leisurely

but still chockful of history, old cars, and conversations with many of the roadside entrepreneurs who helped make Route 66 special. Available from KTCA-TV, 172 E. 4th Street, St. Paul, Minnesota 55101.

Bagdad Café, produced by Percy and Elianor Adlon for Island Pictures. Movie released in 1988, now available from Virgin Vision on videocassette. Superb story told with great humor and compassion. If Dante Alighieri just could have lightened up a bit, he'd have loved this film. Next time you pass a video store, don't go home without it.

Roadhouse 66, produced by Scott M. Rosenfeld and Mark Levinson. Movie distributed in 1984 through Atlantic Releasing, now available from CBS Fox on videocassette. Imagine an American biker script made by a foreign film crew. Now imagine that movie shot on location in the Arizona desert. If you imagined *Animal House Meets the Hell's Angels,* you were close.

Organizations

National organizations of interest to Route 66 travelers include these:

> Route 66 Association
> P.O. Drawer 5323
> Oxnard, CA 93031

> Society for Commercial Archeology
> National Museum of American History
> Room 5010
> Washington, D.C. 20560

Along the route, active statewide associations currently include the following:

> Route 66 Association of Illinois
> 1208 W. Edwards
> Springfield, Illinois 62704

Route 66 Association of Missouri
P.O. Box 8117
St. Louis, Missouri 63156

Oklahoma Route 66 Association
P.O. Box 166
Oklahoma City, Oklahoma 73102

Old Route 66 Association of Texas
P.O. Box 66
McLean, Texas 79057

New Mexico Route 66 Association
P.O. Drawer Q
Gallup, New Mexico 87305

Historic Route 66 Association of Arizona
P.O. Box 66
Kingman, Arizona 86402

AN INVITATION FROM THE AUTHOR

Dear Route 66 Traveler:

American highways are always changing, being redirected, realigned, rebuilt. And Route 66, more than most, is evolving rapidly now as interest in the old road increases.

As this guide goes to press, it is based on the most reliable sources of information available. But words and maps are only approximations of continuing experience, at best. As time passes, corrections and additions will be needed. And I'd like to personally invite you to become a part of that process.

Where you encounter a change in the highway or its roadside attractions, or you find something amiss in this guide, please jot a few lines and drop them in the mail. *Especially* if you find a really good place to eat, or discover some new and wonderful monstrosity, or enjoy a particularly friendly place. Time and the press of other projects may not allow me to answer each suggestion personally. But you will be acknowledged. And when a second edition is planned, your contribution can be of great value.

Your fellow roadies will appreciate your participation and so will I. Thanks for taking the time to make the Route 66 experience even better.

Warm regards,

Tom Snyder

Mailing Address:
Route 66 Traveler's Guide
Post Office Drawer 5323
Oxnard, California 93031

Index